D1598465

SOMETHING LIKE HORACE

SOMETHING
LIKE
HORACE

Studies in the Art and Allusion of
Pope's Horatian Satires

JOHN M. ADEN

VANDERBILT UNIVERSITY PRESS · 1969

Copyright © 1962, 1967, 1969
John M. Aden

Standard Book Number 8265–1138–4

Library of Congress Catalogue
Card Number 71–83208

*Printed in the United States of America by
Kingsport Press, Inc., Kingsport, Tennessee*

To

MARIE

in lieu of many ornaments

Abbreviations

Sources Frequently Referred to in the Notes

Bowles   William Lisle Bowles, ed., *The Works of Alexander Pope, Esq.,* 10 vols. London, 1806.

Butt   John Butt, ed., *Imitations of Horace,* Vol. IV in The Twickenham Edition of *The Poems of Alexander Pope.* London: Methuen, 1939.

Corr.   *The Correspondence of Alexander Pope,* ed. George Sherburn, 5 vols. Oxford: Clarendon, 1956.

E–C   *The Works of Alexander Pope,* ed. the Rev. Whitwell Elwin and W. J. Courthope, 10 vols. London, 1871–1889.

Griffith   Reginald H. Griffith, *Alexander Pope: A Bibliography,* 2 vols. London: Holland Press, 1962.

Hervey   *Lord Hervey's Memoirs,* ed. Romney Sedgwick. London: William Kimber, 1952.

Horace   *Horace. Satires, Epistles and Ars Poetica* (The Loeb Classical Library), ed. H. Rushton Fairclough. London, 1955.

Rogers   Robert W. Rogers, *The Major Satires of Alexander Pope* (Illinois Studies in Language and Literature, Vol. XL). Urbana: University of Illinois Press, 1955.

Spence   Joseph Spence, *Observations, Anecdotes, and Characters of Books and Men,* ed. James M. Osborn, 2 vols. Oxford: Clarendon, 1966.

Warton   Joseph Warton, ed., *The Works of Alexander Pope, Esq.,* 9 vols. London, 1797.

Contents

Preface

ONLY in the last decade, or slightly better, have the Horatian imitations emerged from the neglect and disrepute of very nearly their whole history. Doubly damned in the romantic rejection of Pope and satire alike—itself a heritage of the Wartonian verdict and the triumph of sublimity—the imitations have, with meagre exception, languished in all but Cimmerian gloom until the middle of our own century.

In 1939 the Twickenham edition afforded a basis for re-study and re-evaluation, but it was not until the mid-fifties that much came of it. At that time Robert W. Rogers, in an epochal study of *The Major Satires of Alexander Pope*, vindicated the reputation of these forgotten poems. Since then they have enjoyed steadily mounting notice in journals and *Festschriften* by such scholars as R. E. Hughes, G. K. Hunter, and Aubrey Williams. Meanwhile, passing notice of them has intensified in books about Pope's poetry as a whole, most recently by such authors as G. Wilson Knight, Reuben Brower, and Thomas R. Edwards Jr. But it was not until 1966 that a book-length study of the imitations at last made an appearance, Thomas Maresca's *Pope's Horatian Poems,* an important study of the theological implications and strategy of five of the poems.

The present book is an attempt to extend this frontier a little further, especially into such still uncharted territory as that of *Satires* II. ii (Bethel), I. ii (*Sober Advice*), *Epistle* I. vi (Murray), and the two imitations in the manner of Swift (*Satire* II. vi and *Epistle* I. vii). Three of its chapters have appeared, in slightly different form, elsewhere: Chapter I, originally titled "Pope and the Satiric Adversary," in *Studies in*

English Literature, II (1962), 267–286 (reprinted in *Essential Articles for the Study of Alexander Pope,* edited by Maynard Mack, 1964; revised, 1968); Chapter III, originally titled "That Impudent Satire: Pope's *Sober Advice,*" in the Dougald Mac-Millan *Festschrift* number of *Studies in Philology,* Extra Series, No. 4 (January 1967), 88–106; and Chapter VI, originally titled "Pope and the Receit to Make a Satire," in *Satire Newsletter,* V (Fall 1967), 25–33. To the editors of these journals, and to my honored teacher and friend, Dougald MacMillan, whom I am pleased thus doubly to salute, I am grateful for their making possible the reprinting, with slight alterations, of these essays.

My indebtedness to the trail-blazing of others in this west-ward movement of Pope studies will be apparent in what follows and will not, I hope, go expressly unacknowledged where appropriate. I am grateful to Mrs. Alberta Martin for her time and care in the typing of my manuscript, to Mr. Daniel Marsteller for his assistance in reading copy and proof, and to my colleague, Professor James J. Stathis, for the benefit of his conversation on the subject. Finally, I am grateful for the opportunity to dedicate this book to one whose devotion to it, and to its author, has been more, no doubt, by far than either deserves.

John M. Aden

SOMETHING LIKE HORACE

The Satiric Adversary

Quisquis es, o modo quem ex adverso dicere feci.
Persius, *Satire* I

OF the devices of formal satire, few are used more sparingly or more effectively by Pope than that of the *adversarius,* or interlocutor of the satiric dialogue. Though neither Pope nor his Roman predecessors made extensive use of it, its advantages proved considerable, especially in the rhetorical design of the satire, and particularly for Pope, who capitalized them beyond the example of his models. The dialogue itself permits an enlivening of the satiric discourse, a diversification of style, tone, and statement; promotes dramatic immediacy; and affords at least the appearance of objectivity. Where the interlocutor is friendly, the poet benefits by the presence of a second satirist on the scene. Where he is antagonistic, he furnishes concrete evidence of the satirist's provocation and specific justification of his contention, *difficile est satiram non scribere.* When corruption is added to antagonism, the adversary provides the satirist an especially effective means of establishing the ethical proof so important to his rhetorical purposes, enhancing, by the contrast he makes, the image of the satirist as *vir bonus,* manifestly superior to the dull, vicious, or naïve fellow contending with him.

3

Some account of the use of this formula in the Roman *satura* will help to further its definition and provide a context in which Pope's performance can be measured and appreciated. Horace, who used it more than any other, used it little. Of his eighteen satires (*sermones*), only five, or something less than a third, are dialogues between Horace and a specific, participating interlocutor or adversary: II. i (Trebatius), II. iii (Damasippus), II. iv (Catius), II. vii (Davus), and II. viii (Fundanius). Though *Satire* II. v is a dialogue, the satirist is not involved, except as creator of the fictional conversation between Ulysses and Tiresias. The fact that with one exception (I. ix. *Ibam forte via Sacra*) Horace employed no dialogue (and hence no adversary) until his second book is interesting, suggesting as it does his own late recognition of the possibilities of the form. Even I.ix is not fundamentally a dialogue, but rather the *report* of a dialogue between the persecuted satirist and a bore who has cornered him. The dramatic immediacy of the piece is undercut by its narrative frame in the imperfect tense. But Horace had caught the idea and continued to experiment with it in the second book.

In II. i he conceives, in Trebatius, a brilliant example of the friendly adversary, in this case a close-mouthed, discreet, and somewhat cynical professional advisor, who, though opposing the satirist, does so for his own good. In II. iii he hits upon the principle of a more vulnerable adversary, Damasippus, the chap who had found salvation in Stoicism and wanted Horace to share in its benefits. But, as happens in almost all Horace's remaining examples, the dialogue machinery barely manages to sustain itself, for Damasippus dominates the discourse and delivers a long stoic lecture repeated from his master Stertinius. Much the same thing happens in II. iv, for example, where Catius, the Epicurean, is allowed to dominate the satire with an extended monologue on the gastronomic niceties of the day.

In II.vii the dialogue is with Davus, Horace's slave, who receives his master's permission to speak out on the occasion of the Saturnalia. Here the interlocutor more nearly approximates the hostility implied in the term *adversary*, but the pattern of interior monologue emerging from the conversational frame recurs in II. viii, where Fundanius, a friendly adversary (if an adversary at all, in any real sense of the word), reports to Horace the absurdities of a dinner party (*cena*) given by Nasidienus Rufus. Dialogue has only token existence, Horace merely leading his friend out to tell about the banquet, for which purpose he takes only nine of the ninety-five lines of the poem.

Of Horace's examples, then, only three present a clear-cut adversary, those involving Trebatius, Damasippus, and Davus; and of these only Davus is overtly hostile. Damasippus turns the charge of madness against Horace only in his last brief speech, and Trebatius is friend and mentor, who opposes the satirist out of concern for his welfare (or, as it may be, out of his cynical indifference to the satirist's crusade). Furthermore, Horace's practice furnishes only one example (II. i) of a genuinely sustained dialogue, his formula tending toward the monologic structure most characteristic of Roman satire. Horace's normal procedure is by means of brief opening dialogue to trigger a protracted monologue on the part of the adversary, whom, when he has overextended himself, Horace trips up or rebuffs in a deft resumption of dialogue.

Juvenal is even less disposed than Horace to dialogue structure. Of his sixteen satires, only two involve the presence of a second person on the satiric scene—the Third and the Ninth—and of these the former scarcely qualifies as a dialogue. Juvenal's temperament, so much more positive than Horace's, was not the kind to experiment with ironic modes and techniques. Even III, though two persons are involved, is not a true dialogue, for the satirist merely reports what his friend Umbricius said to him on the occasion of his leaving the ignoble strife of Rome. Once Umbricius's speech begins, at line 21, the satire reverts to a monologue of 300 lines. *Satire* IX is a genuine dialogue, the satirist speaking four times and at intervals throughout the poem, but it does not involve an adversary, for Naevolus is a suppliant, seeking a shoulder to cry on and a way out of his predicament.

Persius is the only one of the three great Roman satirists to employ an adversary between whom and the satirist there exists genuine tension or opposition, and he is the only one to make his adversary notably naïve or intellectually corrupt. Persius, it is plain, is much more strongly disposed toward dialogue than either Horace or Juvenal, for though only two of his six satires exhibit a definite participating adversary (I and III), nearly all of them strain in that direction, making greater use of what I may call a "nonce" or purely rhetorical adversary than either his predecessor or his successor.

In I, Persius pits himself against a defender of the effete and decadent literary taste of the day, a fellow who by his protests in behalf of the new mode and against the manly and satiric bent of the old, furnishes the satirist the targets against which to let fly his arrows of disdain and rebuke. At the same time, the adversary affords the satirist manifest proof to his audience that the satirist is not merely shadow-boxing when he registers his complaints against the corrupt modern: *ecce homo*. Satire I is a sustained dialogue, with the satirist matching speech for speech his adversary, and the tone of annoyance and disapproval is pronounced throughout. In *Satire* III, however, Persius also regresses in the direction of monologue, dominating the discourse with the young derelict who is his adversary and eventually delivering a lecture to the slugabed, who is permitted to speak only long enough to reveal his indisposition to get up of a morning and force himself into any worthwhile activity.

Persius strengthens the image and function of both roles in the dialogue, that of the satirist in terms of his more nearly equal participation in the conversation and his more caustic attitude and speech, and that of the adversary in terms of his more noticeable antagonism or culpability. In these respects Pope more nearly resembles him than he does either Horace, whom he ostensibly imitates, or Juvenal, with whom he has very little in common at all. Like Persius, Pope keeps dialogue distinct, consistently sets the interlocutor at odds with himself (if sometimes only apparently so), makes capital of the corrupt adversary, manifests a spirit of impatience or contempt, and speaks with a bitter tongue. But he learned much from Horace too, especially in the uses of the friendly adversary and in the strategy of irony. Only occasionally does he rise to the *genus grande* of Juvenalian style, though when he does it is powerful indeed. But in respect to dialogue Juvenal had nothing to contribute.

Quantitatively, Pope's use of the dialogue-adversary technique is about par with the Roman. Exclusive of the odes (IV.i and ix) and the *Ethic Epistles,* and including those poems "Something like Horace," Pope's Horatian poems—which is to say, his formal verse satires—number thirteen. Of these, four, or about one third, employ dialogue with a participating adversary: *The First Satire of the Second Book of Horace, Imitated* (February 1732–33), *An Epistle from Mr. Pope to Dr. Arbuthnot* (January 1734–35), and the two dialogues of the *Epilogue to the Satires* (May and July 1738).

Pope's first dialogue was an imitation of Horace, composed in "two mornings,"[1] when he was confined in early 1732–33 with a fever: "Lord Bolingbroke, [who] came to see me, happened to take up a Horace that lay on the table, and in turning it over dipped on the First Satire of the Second Book. He observed how well that would hit my case, if I were to imitate it in English."[2] The adversary Pope imitated in that satire was Trebatius, "one

1. Letter to Swift 16 February 1732–33. See *Corr.,* III, 348. See also the letters to Richardson (III, 350) and Caryll (III, 353).
2. Spence, I, 143. For the reasons why it "would hit my case," see Rogers, pp. 66 ff. Essentially the point is that after the scandal aroused by the portrait of Timon in the *Epistle to Burlington,* Pope could benefit by a defence in the manner of Horace.

of the most considerable lawyers of his time,"[3] a terse and
unillusioned advisor to the satirist, whose problem was what to
do about the complaints leveled against his satire. To the satirist's "quid faciam," Trebatius replies with professional brevity:
"Quiescas." He is even less vocal to the next question. You mean
give up all verse? asks Horace. "Aio." If Horace is sleepless, let
him oil himself, swim thrice across the Tiber, and meet the night
with plentiful wine. If he must write, let him celebrate Caesar.
When Trebatius adds, "multa laborum/praemia laturus," it is
hard to say whether he is venturing a sly joke or speaking quite
soberly. Upon Horace's observation that it is not easy to gain the
ear of Caesar, Trebatius remarks that even so it is better to try
than to go about offending Pantolabus and Nomentanus or
exciting hostility generally. To Horace's insistence that he is
provoked and that, come what may, he must write, Trebatius
counters, perhaps with a show of sardonic humor, My boy, you
will die young! Some great one will deal you a killing frost.
When Horace appeals to the example of Lucilius, Trebatius
merely reminds him that there are laws against libel. But, pleads
Horace, if the verses be good, if Caesar approve, if the provocation be just and the satirist blameless? Why then, concludes
Trebatius, "Solventur risu tabulae, tu missus abibis."

Trebatius is a good lawyer, wise in the ways of the world, and
perhaps uncommonly close-mouthed for his profession. His con-
tribution to the dialogue is, unlike that of most of Horace's
interlocutors, slight, amounting to about seventeen of the satire's
eighty-six verses. His remarks are not devoid of humor of a wry
kind, but they are never playful, and their humor arises more
from the chance of what is said than from any design on the part
of the speaker to be witty. Trebatius is a kind of cynical *eiron*, a
foil to the *alazoneia* of the eager satirist. He is one of Horace's

3. Pope to Fortescue 18 February 1732–33. *Corr.*, III, 351. C. Trebatius
Testa was friend and correspondent of Cicero.

subtlest adversaries, serving not only in the end to "authorize" Horace's satire, but in the course of the poem to intensify its indictment by juxtaposing to Horace's idealistic principle his own expedient one.

In his adaptation, Pope retains the cautionary character of Trebatius but puts the adversary more in key with himself: witty, sympathetic, and, at heart, as much satirically inclined as the satirist. Pope's Fortescue[4] is more personable and lively than Trebatius, and a somewhat more talkative advisor. He speaks some thirty-four and a half of Pope's 156 verses, or something less than a fourth of the whole. The difference is not great, but one is sensible of it. The real change, however, is in the personality and attitude of the speaker.

Fortescue begins almost as tersely as Trebatius (as much as the difference in languages would allow), pronouncing to the Roman's *Quiescas*, "I'd write no more." But then, unlike Trebatius, he warms to the problem and becomes witty where the Roman was matter-of-fact. If Pope is sleepless and if fools rush into his head, he could nevertheless do nothing worse than to write:

> Why, if the Nights seem tedious—take a Wife;
> Or rather truly, if your Point be Rest,
> Lettuce and Cowslip Wine; *Probatum est.*
> But talk with *Celsus, Celsus* will advise
> Hartshorn, or something that shall close your Eyes.[5]

4. Fortescue was not designated in any of Pope's editions, which carried only the initial L for the adversary. Warburton is responsible for the designation of Fortescue. See *Corr.*, III. 351*n*. Warburton was not without authority, however. In a letter to Fortescue (above, *n*. 3) Pope wrote: "have you seen my imitation of Horace? I fancy it will make you smile; but though, when I first began it, I thought of you; before I came to end it, I considered it might be too ludicrous, to a man of your situation and grave acquaintance, to make you Trebatius. . . ." Cf. also the note on the MS. reading of "Hollins," Fortescue's doctor, for Celsus (v. 19), in E-C, IX, 133.

5. Vv. 16–20. Hereafter line numbers will be cited in the text.

By comparison with Trebatius' essentially sober advice, this is a
tissue of witticism and bawdy and refuses to take the question of
the satirist (*quid faciam?*) quite seriously, perhaps because it
recognizes that the satirist himself is not quite serious. It jests on
the use of wives for sleeplessness and, almost certainly, on the
poet's lack of qualification for that remedy. It then wittily turns
on that jest and breaks another upon it—that, on second
thought, a wife may not be the best remedy for restlessness after
all. A sleeping potion then! Professor Butt reminds us of the
anaphrodisiac properties of lettuce and of the likelihood of
whimsicality in the prescription of hartshorn, a stimulant rather
than a soporific.[6]

When he comes to Trebatius' advice, Write of Caesar, at
which the Roman may have winked in *multa laborum/praemia
laturus*, Fortescue spells out the ludicrous possibilities: "You'll
gain at least a *Knighthood*, or the *Bays*." In the time of a
Walpole and a Cibber, neither of these rewards could be taken
seriously (even if Pope were not a Catholic) and in suggesting
them Fortescue is given another function Horace did not confer
upon Trebatius—that of fellow satirist. While he pretends to
counsel discretion, Fortescue joins in the game and contributes
to the satire, not only here, but in his next suggestion:

> Then all your Muse's softer Art display,
> Let Carolina smooth the tuneful Lay,
> Lull with *Amelia's* liquid Name the Nine,
> And sweetly flow through all the Royal Line.

A vein of irony and ridicule runs through this advice, which is
all but open in its contempt for the royal household. Such
audacity was scarcely available to Horace, even had he been
inclined to it. As for Trebatius, he was incapable of it, either by
temperament or by policy.

Even when he tries to be earnest, Fortescue cannot resist

6. Butt, notes pp. 5–6.

slyness: "Better be *Cibber*, I'll maintain it still,/Than ridicule all *Taste*, blaspheme *Quadrille*" (37–38). Here he alludes to Pope's *Epistle to Burlington* and *Epistle to Bathurst*, which, he suggests, with tongue in cheek, it is better to forego and follow instead the insipid panegyrism of Laureate Cibber. By now, too, it becomes apparent that Fortescue is consistently naming the names he advises his friend to avoid. He continues to do so in his next comment, which is, at the same time, the most nearly serious statement he makes in the entire dialogue:

> A hundred smart in *Timon* and in *Balaam*:
> The fewer still you name, you wound the more;
> *Bond* is but one, but *Harpax* is a Score.
>
> [42–44]

It should not escape notice either that in the reference to Timon, Fortescue is obliquely countering the charge that by that character the poet meant the Duke of Chandos. Fortescue is adversary in name only; he is in reality the poet's ally, and we see him progress from Pope's counsellor to his advocate to his fellow satirist.

When, like Horace, Pope says, "I will Rhyme and Print" (Horace had said only *scribam*), Fortescue almost translates Trebatius: "Alas, young Man! your Days can ne'r be long." But then he lapses into his facetious mood again: "In Flow'r of Age you perish for a Song." Where Trebatius let the jest, if it were a jest, go with "O puer," Fortescue, having said "young man," instantly perceives that he speaks to a friend nearly forty-five years old, and so corrects himself with a witty play on the cliché "flower of youth," and perhaps a pleasantry at his friend's expense as well. Unlike Trebatius, he will specify the potential enemies and continue his participation in the satire he pretends to decry: "Plums, and Directors, *Shylock* and his wife,/Will club their Testers, now, to take your Life!" To Pope's plea about provocation, virtue, and friendship with the great, Fortescue explains: "Your Plea is good. But still I say, beware!/Laws are explain'd by Men—so have a care." Trebatius had merely called attention to the existence of the law. Fortescue remembers the jurists, who, he would seem to say, are more crucial to the issue than the laws. He continues:

> It stands on record, that in *Richard's* Time
> A Man was hang'd for very honest Rhymes.
> Consult the Statute: *quart.* I think it is,
> *Edwardi Sext.* or *prim.* & *quint. Eliz:*
> See *Libels, Satires*—here you have it—read.
>
> [145–149]

Several things are noteworthy about this. For one, Fortescue gives us a glimpse of himself as a professional man in a way that Trebatius does not. He knows the cases, the statutes; at least he can make a good show at ransacking his memory and his books. He is, in other words, more real than Trebatius because more circumstantial in his self-display. And Fortescue displays his legal skill, his rhetorical subtlety in word play, as in the case of *honest,* which, though it seems to concede the point of criminal frankness associated with satire, at the same time asserts the ideas of virtue, uprightness, and sincerity. But even more important in the economy of the poem is the suggestion which this speech affords of the setting which Miss Randolph reminds us lurks somewhere in the background of the typical *satura,* though Horace's poem seems to lack it.[7] The advantage in Pope's case is considerable, placing as it does the satirist and his respected interlocutor on a familiar, easy, and dignified footing. Fortescue has a book in hand, opens it to the appropriate places, hands it to his friend to read for himself. From this arises a distinct impression of scene—the only one in the poem, though it reaches back at once and gathers in the rest of the dialogue—and the reassur-

7. Mary Claire Randolph, "The Structural Design of Formal Verse Satire," *PQ,* XXI (1942), 372.

ances, both dramatic and ethical, which that promotes. It is as if poet and friend are come together in the friend's chambers or study, talk with the intimacy and frankness of witty companions, handle the books that surround them, and enjoy a problem and a jest together. The effect is to make seem private, and hence more candid, what is, in actuality, quite public.

The poet will leave this scene with good advice, but with something more important even than that. Fortescue's last speech, dismissing the case, is in Trebatius' low key, but adds a significant point. To Horace's proposal of a hypothetically justi- fied case of satire, Trebatius says only that the satirist might expect to have a case against him dismissed. Fortescue tells his poet, "you may then *proceed*."[8] He does more than exonerate the satirist; he gives him his blessing and his leave to carry on.

Pope has heightened and complicated the adversary he bor- rowed from Horace. His Fortescue enlivens the dialogue with his own wit, contributes more or less openly to the satire he purports to warn against, defines himself as a personality, pro- vides an effective suggestion of setting, and, at the last, renders an opinion that doesn't just get the satirist *off*, but that encour- ages him to *get on*—with his work. Horace pits himself against a stubborn adversary and wrings from him a concession at best; Pope recruits a partisan, who shares his ideals, adds the force of his reputation and wit into the bargain, and sanctions his perse- verance in the cause. Pope's adversary has, without sacrificing any of the tensional value of Horace's, become a powerful ally. Like Arbuthnot, Fortescue stands revealed, despite his pose, "To Virtue only and Her Friends, a Friend."[9]

8. Italics mine.
9. It should not go unnoticed that Fortescue is the friend of Walpole as well as of Pope. This may be another reason Pope decided against naming him as the adversary. But the identity was undoubtedly an open secret, so that Pope could have it both ways. The advantage of such an adversary—a friend in court—is considerable and was almost certainly calculated.

I include the *Epistle to Arbuthnot* among the poems employ-
ing an adversary because, even though as originally published no
adversary was identified, I believe a case can be made for Warburton's procedure in giving some of the speeches to Arbuthnot
in the 1751 edition of the *Works*.[10] Normally, it is true, the
epistle, as a form, does not employ an interlocutor, that presumably being a contradiction in terms. According to Acron, *epistulis
ad absentes loquimur, sermone cum praesentibus*.[11] None of
Horace's *Epistles* admits a participating adversary, though they
often create, within the framework of the epistle, what I have
called a nonce adversary, for the purpose of rhetorical question

10. Butt, pp. 93–94, summarizes the changes made in the text by Warburton. Although Butt allows that the "change from epistle to dialogue may be
the work of Pope," he regards it as "a change for the worse," and restores the
poem to its earlier epistolary form. Rogers, pp. 70–71, traces in detail the
piecemeal career of the poem's composition, from which it becomes clear that
there is a sufficient confusion surrounding the origins, manuscripts, and texts
of the poem to warrant an open mind on the subject of the form. See also
Pope's letter to Arbuthnot 25 August 1734, *Corr.*, III, 428.

The arguments against dialogue structure boil down to the fact that (1) the
poem is entitled an "epistle," (2) in none of the MSS. or texts supervised by
Pope is an interlocutor designated by rubric. In favor of dialogue structure
(or, more properly, of *mixed* structure) may be urged (1) the presence of
quotation marks at every point later identified by Warburton as Arbuthnot's
interjection (that there are quotation marks elsewhere is no hindrance, for
they are all clearly associated with some identified speaker), (2) the correla-
tion of the speeches later assigned to Arbuthnot with his advice to Pope in the
letter of 17 July 1734 (see *Corr.*, III, 417, and Pope's replies, 419–420,
423–424, 428, 431), and (3) the "lead-in" to the first speech assigned to
Arbuthnot. Pope has just said, vv. 73–74, "And is not mine, my Friend, a
sorer case,/When ev'ry Coxcomb perks them in my face?" when the reply
follows, vv. 75 ff. Since there can be no doubt that the "Friend" of verse 73 is
Arbuthnot, there can be no doubt that the speech beginning v. 75 is
Arbuthnot's. This identification is in all likelihood sustained in the "Friend"
mentioned in the second speech, v. 102. None of the other three speeches
assigned to Arbuthnot carries such an identifying vocative, but since all other
quotations in the poem are assigned to some specified speaker (in the nonce
category), there is reason to give these to the Friend who has spoken, in the
same vein, twice before.

11. Quoted in Horace, p. xxi.

and answer.[12] In Pope, such a nonce adversary is very common, and what no doubt began as such in Pope's original wrestling with the poem may have given way to the introduction of his correspondent as, in effect, a present or participating adversary. What more likely happened is that Pope felt the attraction of both forms, the epistle and the dialogue, and admitted a confusion of form into his poem. Not that the result is damaging, for I cannot agree with Professor Butt that the shift to dialogue is "a change for the worse," though it admittedly introduces a contradiction in technical point of view that is somewhat troublesome. Theoretically, an epistle, being a monologue, cannot be a dialogue. The fact remains that Pope seems to have made it not only possible but successful.

Partly, one supposes, by virtue of Pope's hesitancy in the decision, partly by virtue of the quantitatively small part assigned the adversary (Arbuthnot speaks only thirteen and one half of the poem's 419 verses), Pope's second interlocutor does not attain the reality of his first, remaining on the whole, rather like Trebatius, a disembodied voice.[13] This relative shadowiness of figure is amply compensated for, however, by the adversary's trenchancy and audacity, which are quite enough to bring him alive and to distinguish him from the abstracter nonce adversary. Pope must have realized all along the value of having Arbuthnot on the scene, having his own say rather than merely serving as a puppet for Pope's ventriloquism, for the former is precisely the impression the speeches assigned to Arbuthnot make, that of a

12. Cf. Horace's "Si quis nunc quaerat 'quo res haec pertinet?'" (I. ii. 23), "Nunc aliquis dicat mihi: 'quid tu?'" (I. iii. 19), "ecce,/Crispinus minimo me provocat . . ." (I. iv. 13–14). The nonce adversary is in fact the most common form, either in epistolary or satiric writing, and is apparently the basis of Miss Randolph's generalization about the *adversarius* in formal verse satire.

13. Perhaps not utterly disembodied, for he alludes to his height ("I too could write, and I am twice as tall," v. 103). This, as we perceive, is an allusion to Pope's height too, and evokes an image of the two friends side by side, the smaller proving the more heroic.

present interlocutor, reasoning, sympathizing, and ultimately collaborating with the poet.

When the adversary speaks, he does so as the anxious friend, solicitous of the satirist's well-being. He exhibits none of Fortescue's facetiousness or playfulness, but when he lends himself, like Fortescue, to the very cause he decries, he does so with an edge not found in the speech of the earlier adversary. His first remark is in reply to the satirist's question whether, like Midas's Queen, he must not speak out:

> "Good friend forbear! you deal in dang'rous things,
> "I'd never name Queens, Ministers, or Kings;
> "Keep close to Ears, and those let Asses prick,
> "Tis nothing" . . .
>
> [75–78]

The advice is good, and it is urged sincerely, but it has a sting too and a daring innuendo—"Keep close to Ears, and those let Asses prick." One recalls that it was "*Midas,* a sacred Person and a King," who had the ass's ears, and he realizes that it is unnecessary to await the *Augustus* to see a satirist bite his thumb at a King. The satirist is shrewd enough in this instance, however, to let a great and respected public figure do the biting for him. "Tis nothing" is also finely ambiguous and teasing, and ought not to go unnoticed.

The adversary's next interruption is a warning against the use of personal names and a reminder that the satirist is physically vulnerable to retaliation:

> . . . "Hold! for God-sake—you'll offend:
> "No Names—be calm—learn Prudence of a Friend:
> "I too could write, and I am twice as tall,
> "But Foes like these!". . .
>
> [101–104][14]

14. Cf. Arbuthnot's letter to Pope 17 July 1734, and Pope's reply 26 July 1734 (*Corr.,* III, 417, 419–420).

Again good advice followed by the advisor's own stroke, scarcely disguised, for the foes are the names Pope has just mentioned: *Colly, Henley, Moor* [James Moore-Smythe], *Phillips,* and *Sapho;* and "like these" admits of indefinite construction along unflattering lines. When he advises prudence, moreover, Arbuthnot is doing what every friendly adversary does, that is, more than he reckons; for he is not only counselling wisdom, but in so doing, providing a mark by which the satirist's superiority to convenience may be measured.

When Sporus is mentioned, the adversary cannot suppress his contempt, and his advice to let Sporus alone is itself an attack upon him: "What? that Thing of silk,/*Sporus,* that mere white Curd of Ass's milk?/Satire or Sense alas! can Sporus feel?/Who breaks a butterfly upon a Wheel?" By means of his adversary Pope can have it both ways, can express the feeling that Hervey is beneath contempt and yet have at him all the same, all the while gaining the sanction of an Arbuthnot.

Two further interjections by the adversary are quite brief and function merely to provide the needed questions: "But why insult the Poor, affront the Great?" (v. 360), enabling the poet to proclaim "A Knave's a Knave, to me, in ev'ry State"; and a final question, "What Fortune, pray?" (v. 390), enabling him to distinguish the means of his family from the ill-gotten gains of others.

Whether the concluding couplet of the poem belongs to Arbuthnot or to Pope must remain a conjecture. Warburton assigned it to Arbuthnot, and it is certainly more effective as his than as Pope's, but lacking quotation marks in any of the editions Pope sponsored, it cannot with the same confidence be assigned to him. As Arbuthnot's, it would show the adversary persuaded by the satirist's argument and in effect, like Fortescue, endorsing it, proclaiming, moreover, that ultimate judgment of the poet belongs to Heaven, not to his enemies: "Whether that

Blessing be deny'd, or giv'n,/Thus far was right, the rest belongs to Heaven."[15]

In some respects, Pope's second adversary retains the character and functions of his first: both are friendly adversaries, opposing the satirist for his own good; both participate in the satire while ostensibly opposing it; and both (if the last couplet of the *Epistle* does belong to Arbuthnot) pronounce an exoneration of the satirist. But in other respects Arbuthnot differs from Fortescue, and one is left with the impression of unique personality in Pope's friendly adversaries. Gone now is the facetiousness of Fortescue, his witty jibes at the common foe, his easy rapport with the satirist, and in its place is a bluntness, a sarcasm, and a fierceness matching that of the satirist himself. This is partly the effect, as I have suggested, of his being Arbuthnot rather than Fortescue. But it must be acknowledged an effect too of a reflex in Pope's technique with the friendly adversary, for what has happened is that the adversary has changed character along with the satirist. The friendly adversary in Pope is partly an alter ego. What really changes is the satirist, and the adversary is accommodated to the change. Pope is now more tart, more indignant —more himself and less Horatian—than he was in the Imitation, and the adversary reflects this shift in point of view. In both poems the adversary works with and for the poet, but how he does so is dictated partly by his identity as a person, partly by the satirist's peculiar disposition in each poem. As far as this affects the *Epistle to Arbuthnot*, it may provide additional explanation of the reduced scale of the adversary's participation. Pope is rather too heated on this occasion to allow his adversary much

15. Part of the difficulty surrounding the interpretation of this couplet stems no doubt from the fact that the final paragraph of the *Epistle*, like other parts of it, was one of the pieces of earlier vintage brought together to form the "Bill of Complaint" published 2 January 1734–35 as *An Epistle to Dr. Arbuthnot*. A version of these verses was written as early as 3 September 1731 and included in a letter to Aaron Hill (*Corr.*, III, 226–227). This version may also be consulted in Butt, p. 127n.

intervention. When he does admit him, though, he has him lay about to good and solid effect.

Pope's final, and consummate, experiment with the adversary occurs in the two dialogues of the *Epilogue to the Satires*, both composed and published in the spring and summer of 1738. In these poems he makes the adversary a genuinely hostile figure, introduces a new dimension of irony, and translates the interlocutor into a symbol of the whole satiric indictment.

Dialogue I (originally titled *One Thousand Seven Hundred and Thirty Eight. A Dialogue Something like Horace*) is essentially an ironic structure in which Pope permits a corrupt adversary to dissuade (or seem to dissuade) him from a defense of satire and to talk (or seem to talk) him into an ostensible defense of Vice. The relation of the poet to the adversary is thus unique in this poem, both with respect to Pope's earlier and his later practice. In the Imitation (*Satire* II.i) Pope, following Horace, contended with his adversary, who, unlike Horace's, did not really want to dissuade the satirist anyway. In the *Arbuthnot*, though the adversary was more earnest in his efforts to dissuade, he was at the same time more ready to give vent to satire himself. In the second dialogue of the *Epilogue*, satirist and adversary are at genuine sixes and sevens.

The difference is made to arise, properly enough, from the character conferred upon the several adversaries. In the earlier defenses, the adversary was actually friendly to the poet, intelligent, and, if shrewd, nonetheless honest. In Dialogue I the adversary, who is not on Pope's side at all but a true adversary, a symbol of Pope's hostile public and a spokesman for its corrupt principles, is neither friendly, intelligent, nor honest. He is instead somewhat foppish (a Sir Courtly Wit) and presumptuous,[16] a good deal vicious, and not a little stupid: an epitome of the corruption he speaks for. Such a creature has the traits of a

---

16. In Pope's own note (1751) the adversary is characterized as "an impertinent Censurer." See Butt, p. 297.

true *alazon*, blandly unaware of his knack for self-exposure. What more natural, then, than for the satirist to slip into the role of *eiron*, let this fellow extend himself and feel that he is triumphing, while all along the ground is shifting under him and depriving him of footing. No need to argue with a dunce when you can damn him with feigned praise.

The dialogue's effectiveness is ultimately the product of Pope's portrayal and manipulation of this vulnerable adversary. For Pope not only wins the argument, but through the personification of vice and folly in his adversary makes dramatically real the threat to virtue which he proclaims. Part of the "willing World" drawn in "golden Chains" at the wheels of Vice's "Triumphal Car" is the adversary himself, both a victim and a counterpart in the real world of the Vice symbolized in the metaphoric world of the poem. In him the audience may view Vice "her own image, and the very age and body of the time his form and pressure."

The shift to a negatively functioning adversary is marked by several external tokens. The adversary is designated by the conventional rubric "Fr." (Friend), thus generalizing him on the one hand, leaving him undiscriminated from the crowd of time-servers he speaks for, and dissociating him from the poet's acquaintance on the other.[17] Also, contrary to earlier procedure, the adversary is permitted to speak first, a gambit which not only shows him as aggressor but which reveals his character and mentality, both of which maneuver him into a position of immediate vulnerability. Finally, the proportion of the adversary's speaking part is sharply increased over previous examples,[18] the

17. In the first edition (1738) adversary and satirist were designated respectively A and B. Fr. (F.) and P are substituted in 1740. The same is true of Dialogue II.

18. 40.7 per cent of the whole number of verses. Fortescue spoke some 22 per cent of the lines in his poem, Arbuthnot 3.1 per cent of those in his. The adversary of Dialogue II speaks about 8.23 per cent of the verses in that poem.

reason being the satirist's desire to let the fellow damn himself, as he does, with astonishing thoroughness.

The self-indictment begins at once. By opening the dialogue with an echo of Damasippus's rebuke of Horace (*Satire* II.iii. 1–4), the adversary displays a fashionable familiarity with Horace but no sense of the awkwardness of the comparison which he invites by it. For Damasippus is, after all, a zealot, a mere spouter of stoic doctrine, and he proves in the end, with the stoicism he dumps so facilely on Horace, the butt of Horace's ridicule. The adversary's play on Damassipus' lines is made, too, at the expense of strict accuracy regarding the frequency of Pope's publication. In a note to these opening lines, Pope says that they were "meant to give a handle to that which follows in the character of an impertinent Censurer," and there is every reason to suppose that he meant this comment to include such revelations of opaqueness and factual unreliability as we have noted already, or such others in this immediate context as the Friend's revealing comment that, when Pope does publish, "the Court see nothing in't." Damasippus had not designated the Court as the judge of Horace's performance, but had said only *nil dignum sermone canas*: you make no poem worth heeding. If his standard was a fanatical Stoicism, it was at least better than that of Pope's adversary.

But these lines about the Court deserve further notice, for the economy of Pope's technique is nowhere better demonstrated. By the remark the adversary intends no more than that the Court is unimpressed with what the poet has published, but the way he says it and the implications flowing from it are extremely damaging to him and to the opposition he represents. For what the Court does not approve is, among other things, the *Epistle to Augustus,* with its reflections on the King and on the times, a disapproval, therefore, scarcely either candid or moral. But when the adversary words it, "the Court *see* nothing in't," he suggests yet another interpretation—that the Court is not intelligent enough to see what it is that the poet is doing. In their dullness they are left wondering what this poet is writing about. "Why will not my subjects write in prose?"

The Friend continues in this vein, complaining next (of all things!) of the poet's correctness and of his moral bias (which he disallows to Wit), both of which he describes, along with the charge of stealing from Horace, as "Decay of Parts." In such wise does he betray his own and the Court's inverted values. Nor does he enhance the image of his morals and wit by his shallow and palpable attempts at flattering the poet, "who once with Rapture writ."

In the same speech (Pope hasn't spoken yet: why should he?), the adversary confidently commends Horace for all the wrong reasons,[19] for his "sly, polite, insinuating stile," which, he notes, "Could please at Court, and make Augustus smile." He suggests that the satirist follow suit, and recommends specifically the consolation of Sir Robert's "Groat." To the poet's protest that to do so would cost him his laughter, the adversary makes no difficulty of suggesting that he indulge his satiric bent on "Scripture," "Honesty," Patriotism, harmless themes, which "all Lord Chamberlains allow." He may, in fact, vent his satire on any but "Fools or Foes," a suspicious and, one would think, embarrassing set of categories to defend. When the poet ironically yields to this High Argument and bids adieu to Satire, the Friend, who does not recognize when he is well off (the satirist has just consented to lay his satire by), holds out the consolatory suggestion that the poet might still attack those disgraced, already down and out, once again bidding him only spare those in place. All this is tossed off in a brisk, dancing pace that bespeaks the

---

19. The reasons are wrong in terms of Pope's values. It is possible of course that Pope might concur in the notion that Horace was guilty of such faults. Cf. the lines from Dryden's translation of Persius's *Satire* I. 116–118, quoted in Butt, p. 299n. It should be noted that in them Persius's description of Horace seems intended for a compliment.

glib self-assuredness of the "well Whipt Cream of Courtly Sense."

Damaging as it is, however, the adversary's corrupt morality is not perhaps his most vulnerable point. What may be worse, though it is no doubt a symptom of the former, is his mental ineptitude, his touch of stupidity and dullness. He is not only a vicious man, but something of a dunce too, and perhaps Pope wants us to suppose that the two have a way of going together. Here, at any rate, is a spokesman who can accuse the satirist of stealing from Horace (vv. 7 ff.) and then turn around in the next breath and praise Horace and distinguish his manner from that of the satirist (vv. 11 ff.); who in his reply (vv. 37 ff.) to the satirist's remarks on Walpole can himself inadvertently slander the minister; who immediately on the heels of the blunder can put himself in the extremely awkward position of acknowledging the virtue of Lyttleton and of Fleury and of condemning Hervey (Lord Fanny: vv. 45–52); who can express a doctrine so crass (vv. 53–62) that even Vice would blush to own it; and who, finally, can unintentionally damn the very Court he is defending ("There, where no Passion, Pride, or Shame transport," etc., vv. 97–104).

Pope's adversary is still participating in his satire, but unwittingly now, and for that reason all the more effectively. The Friend in Dialogue I, like the *personae* of Swift's satires, is so convinced of his own and his country's normality and of the rightness of their vision that he is incapable of recognizing, or even of conceiving, such a thing as self-incrimination, to say nothing of acknowledging public wrong and ruin. Pope's adversary fulfills the parable: "Out of thine own mouth will I judge thee, wicked Courtier."

Against this corrupt symbol, to whom he stands as positive foil, looms the satirist who is the object of his vicious and clumsy blandishments—the *vir bonus,* but more than that, *vir ingeniosus* as well: a man who can draw the line between Walpole's good and his evil (vv. 27–36); who is witty enough to play the ironist with his adversary, pretending to give up satire (along with "Distinction . . . Warmth, and Truth") and to praise folly; who pretends even to come to the defense of Vice and to safeguard against common use what is rightfully the Court's alone, and who thus shames the nation's leadership, which would debase, not redeem, its stewardship.

The adversary of the second Dialogue, like his noble kinsman in I, is, with slight differences of emphasis, also a self-deceived, morally corrupt *persona*. The difference in the two is to be felt largely in the manner of their exposure. Where in Dialogue I the adversary exposes himself through his stupidity and moral confusion, that in II is tripped up or squarely answered by the poet, who opposes him at every turn, with the exception of two or three momentary instances of ironic pose. The folly of the Friend in II lies more in simple heedlessness and argumentative incaution than in outright stupidity, though he is by no means as mentally alert as he needs to be in order to engage Pope. This defect of carelessness, with its hint of mental sluggishness, is comically exposed near the outset of the poem. In the political vein of his predecessor, the Friend suggests to the satirist that he "Spare . . . the Person, and expose the Vice," with which the poet pretends to comply, only to suck in the adversary. "Ye Statesmen, Priests . . . Ye Tradesmen vile . . . Ye Rev'rend Atheists!" cries the satirist, whereupon the Friend breaks in: "Scandal! Name them, Who?/P. Why that's the thing you bid me not to do." Upon the poet's subsequent allusion to the "pois'ning Dame," the Friend interrupts again:

> Fr. You mean—P. I don't.—Fr.
> You do.
> P. See! now I keep the Secret, and not you.
> The bribing Statesman—Fr. Hold! too high you go.
> P. The Brib'd Elector—Fr. There you stoop too low.
> P. I fain wou'd please you, if I knew with what:
> Tell me, which Knave is lawful Game, which not?

Obviously the Court will have to field a better man than this if it expects to discredit the satirist. The fact that it apparently cannot is not the least of the satirist's proofs against it. Its representative, at any rate, has so far managed only to botch the job: he has revealed the slow wit and inconsistency of his ilk and has proved quite handily the satirist's contention that general satire is ineffective.

If not as obviously depraved as his brother in Dialogue I, the adversary in II nevertheless shares his double standard and, like him, dramatizes the evil the poem decries. He would have the satirist do his victims at least the favor of a dash for anonymity (v. 11). He has, as we have seen, his own taste for scandal, which ironically vitiates his complaints against the satirist. He would spare the man trying to make his way in the world ("You hurt a man that's rising in the Trade," v. 35). He would divert satire to the dead and low-life (Jonathan Wild, v. 54). His whole argument tends, in short, to the worldly comfort of no satire at all.

But while he is on the one hand a temporizer with vice, on the other he functions as the agent of the poet's strictly argumentative needs, raising the right questions to occasion the satirist's defense of his satire. That he raises them for the wrong reasons is but an added effect of the poet's art. If you must satirize, he asks, why must you use names? Why do you return over and over to the same victims? Do you complain of those in power because your friends are out? What is it to you anyway? he asks, his crassness mingling now with the poet's most quiet need. Pope continues to have it both ways. He wanted these questions, needed them, and he met them with strength and wit; but at the same time he got them posed by a fellow basically unprincipled, who, in putting them, inadvertently contributes to the satire himself. But by nothing does Pope more finely discriminate between himself and his adversary (and his adversary's constituency) than by the Friend's objection to the satirist's simile of the Westphaly hogs: "This filthy Simile, this beastly Line,/Quite turns my Stomach . . ." (vv. 181–182). The adversary's is a morality that can stomach vice, but not the image of it.

Against this temporizing figure is balanced once again the image of the poet, standing for the right, with his "strong Antipathy of Good to bad" and his sense of "Affront," which should be the adversary's too. After the poet's great peroration in defense of satire ("O sacred Weapon!" vv. 212–253), the adversary is understandably shaken and draws back in a nervous and feeble attempt to divert the satirist's indignation: "Alas! alas! pray end what you began,/And write next winter more *Essays on Man,*" that is, general, philosophic, personally innocuous satire. The satirist doesn't even bother to notice.

The Friend of Dialogue II has served the satirist as *provocateur,* Machiavel, hypocrite, courtly wit, and inquisitor more helpful than harmful. He has furthered the satire by commending moral relativism, by protesting delicacy in the face of honest scatology but acknowledging stomach enough for flattery, by prodding the satirist into the noblest apology for satire on record, and by betraying the intimidation which must always mark the corrupt in the presence of aroused virtue. From him Pope has extracted the last full measure of collaboration. And that may be one reason, among others, why Pope did not compose other dialogues in the brief time left to him. He had done about all that could be done with the form. He had taken a device scarcely defined in Roman usage—hardly known to Juvenal at all, experimented with cleverly but tentatively by Horace, and only somewhat sharpened in focus by Persius—and made of it a brilliant and versatile accessory of the satiric strategy. He diversified and intensified Horace's precedent in the use of the friendly adversary, and elaborated and extended Persius' in the use of the hostile one. He outstrips the field in the fusion of irony and virulence, in the creation of dramatic tension, and in the assimilation of the adversary into the total satiric economy.

2

The Satiric Prolocutor

THE prolocutor, or spokesman, is a device even rarer in formal satire than the adversary, and one quite singular in Popeian usage. In its purest form, represented by Horace's *Second Satire of the Second Book* and Pope's imitation, the prolocutor is a person, usually historically real, who is introduced, ordinarily though not exclusively by indirect discourse, in the course of a satiric monologue, to speak part, if not most, of its lesson; and who, in various ways, is made to function in behalf of the satirist. He differs from the interlocutor, or adversary, in that the latter is a participant in a dialogue and hence actually present on the scene or at least felt to be so. By definition, too, the adversary is in some kind of tension, if only prudential, with the satirist. The prolocutor, on the other hand, is not present, but is reported by the satiric monologist; and, far from being in tension with the satirist, always, as Pope says, "thinks the very thing he ought," that is, thinks and speaks in complete accord with the satirist, for whom he is in fact the mouthpiece.

It seems likely that the device grew out of the satiric adaptation of the Greek ἀπομνημονεύματα, a mode of popular philosophic exposition in which a pupil reports upon the wisdom, or, it may be, the actions of his master.[1] Lucilius probably made use

1. For an account of the ἀπομνημονεύματα, see George Converse Fiske, *Lucilius and Horace, A Study in the Classical Theory of Imitation* (Wiscon-

of this form of the device, and Horace may or may not have followed his example in such satires as II. iii, iv, and vii.[2] But the prolocutor differs from this *discipulus,* as he may be called, in at least two important ways: the proximity of his association with the satirist and the proximity of his viewpoint with that of the satirist. More often than not, when the *discipulus* figures in a satire, he does so in an adversarial posture. The prolocutor, as we have indicated, is the satirist's guide, philosopher, and friend. Neither persona, it may be added, has much currency in satire. Though Horace seems to have invented the prolocutor, he used it only once. Persius does not use it at all, though he invokes something like it in the opening of his *Fourth,* where Socrates is made to deliver himself briefly on the subject of political pretenders. Juvenal has only Umbricius, who pronounces an elaborate farewell to Rome in the *Third Satire.*

The English history of the device is even more barren. Apart from translations and imitations, it is a history of neglect, if not indifference. In view of the abusive tendency of English satire, especially in its early and middle stages, this is not especially surprising. Indeed, the rarity of prolocutory satire may be due to the fact that, judging by the few specimens and near specimens that we have, it seems almost exclusively adapted to satiric poems basically didactic or philosophic in motive and content: to satire, in other words, that aims more immediately to instruct, or edify, than to attack. Such a motive, like the indirectness of the technique itself, is scarcely natural to the Lucilian temperament, whether Roman or otherwise. Irony and indirection, even philosophic motivation, are more characteristic of the Menippean spirit.[3] The instinct of the Lucilian satirist is to speak *in propria*

---

sin Studies in Language and Literature, No. 7, Madison: The University of Wisconsin Press, 1920), pp. 156–158.

2. *Ibid.*

3. I use *Lucilian* and *Menippean* here to distinguish between what Horace describes on the one hand as *sale multo/urbem defricuit* (*Sat.* I. x. 3–4) and,

persona and directly to the point, a fact which also accounts, we may suppose, for the scarcity of dialogue in formal verse satire. Horace, as I say, verges on the prolocutory formula in his use of the ἀπομνημόνευμα. It is to him, at any rate, the most detached of the Lucilian satirists, that we must turn for the only appreciable record of experimentation with the mode. He first (and strictly speaking last) resorts to the prolocutor in *Sat.* II. ii, the poem Pope adapts to Bethel. After announcing his theme— *Quae virtus et quanta, boni, sit vivere parvo*—he declares that what he will have to say on that subject is not his own lore, but that of the old farmer, Ofellus, *abnormis sapiens crassaque Minerva,* a self-made philosopher. He then proceeds, at least ostensibly, to recite the wisdom of that venerable authority. What follows, until near the end, is an indirect discourse which, while it conveys some impression of the homely speech proper to such a spokesman, makes no effort to create a consistent illusion of such speech. Though the utterances exhibit generally a brevity and even downrightness appropriate to rustic discourse—*siccus, inanis/sperne cibum vilem . . . num vesceris ista/quam laudas pluma?*[4]—Ofellus proves occasionally, by virtue of Horace's casual transmission, not only well spoken but well read:

> . . . . seu pila velox
> molliter austerum studio fallente laborem.
> . . . . haud ita pridem
> Galloni praeconis erat acipensere mensa
> infamis.[5]

---

on the other, as *ridentem dicere verum* (*Sat.* I. i. 24). It is the difference between the punitive and the playful. See my note, "Towards a Uniform Satiric Terminology," *Satire Newsletter,* I (Spring 1964), 30–32.

4. Vv. 14–15 ("dry and hungry, despise, if you can, plain food"), 27–28 ("Now, do you eat the feathers you are so crazy about?"). Fiske (p. 379) relates the quality and method of Ofellus's discourse to the Cynic διατριβαί.

5. Vv. 11–12 ("whether, out of excitement, the swift ball pleasingly lightens the strenuous exercise"), 46–48 ("It was not long since that the table of Gallonius the auctioneer was, by virtue of a sturgeon, rendered infamous").

The style vacillates in this way between the rural and the urbane until, in verse 116, Horace finally commits the wisdom of Ofellus unequivocally to the prolocutor's own words.

This informality of stylistic decorum does not, however, diminish the advantage Horace found, and doubtless sought, in the use of his rural persona, including the obvious one of placing a discourse on simplicity in the mouth of one peculiarly qualified to speak on that subject, one who, perhaps, could not only more safely proclaim it than Horace himself, but who could bring to it the advantage of unassailable authority. Blameless, sensible and sturdy, Ofellus reflects the standard of nature, the infallible testament and the most impressive reproach to luxury.[6]

Given a rural prolocutor, moreover, Horace could avail himself of an idiom often emphatic and convincing in a way that polite speech cannot be, while at the same time, by virtue of the indirect discourse, making such idiom palatable to polite ears by the admixture of a more educated style. By his procedure, in short, Horace was able to have it both ways: forthright and to the point and at the same time intellectually and aesthetically resonant. Even so, when at the end he says, by way of introducing Ofellus's own speech, *Quo magis his credas,* he may be said to have in mind not just the force of fact—that Ofellus practiced what he preached—but the importance of dramatic presence and style, for the direct discourse of Ofellus is eloquent in its simplicity and impressive in its immediacy.[7]

This latter is apparently an allusion to a Lucilian satire on, or touching on, Gallonius (See Fiske, p. 384, and *Remains of Old Latin,* edited and translated by E. H. Warmington [Loeb, 1938], III, 62–65). Ofellus is also made to refer to Terence in *cena dubia* (v. 77), and to philosophic usage in *animum* (v. 78).

6. Fiske observes, p. 379, that it is "a favorite device in the Cynic διατριβαί to oppose the plain, rude peasant, the type of the natural man of the Cynics to the 'high liver.'"

7. Cf. Horace's remark to Catius (*Sat.* II. iv. 90–91) after he has heard the latter's report of a culinary lecture: "though you relate all to me by memory, yet as interpreter you cannot delight me so much [as the man himself]." In this context, of course, the remark is ironic.

Although *Satires* iii, iv and vii of the Second Book restore the prolocutory role to its primitive usage in the ἀπομνημόνευμα, they are helpful in defining the newer function and warrant some brief attention. All three of the satires, it should be noted, are dialogues.

In *Sat.* II. iii Damasippus, a reformed speculator, assails Horace at his Sabine farm, reproaches him for his idleness, and tells him how he was rescued from despair (over his bankruptcy) by Stertinius, whose words of wisdom he proceeds to repeat for the benefit of the unredeemed Horace. At the conclusion of the lecture the dialogue resumes, and Horace first genially twits the new recruit and finally cries him mercy of *his* form of madness. Critics have long recognized that this satire not only canvasses the follies of mankind but at the same time mocks the excesses of Stoic response to those follies. It is no doubt for this reason that Horace chose to work with an adversary rather than a prolocutor. Horace speaks for himself in this satire and reveals himself at odds, if not with Stertinius, with the zealot who throws Stertinius at him. If Stertinius is to be thought of as a prolocutor at all, it must be as prolocutor for Damasippus immediately and for Horace only proximately, from whom he is twice removed and not a little compromised by the middle man.

In *Sat.* II. iv, Catius, an acquaintance and Epicurean, relates to Horace some new points of gastronomical doctrine he has just heard from a lecturer whose name he declines to reveal. Here again we have a lesson with which Horace is not wholly, if at all, in sympathy, so that whatever prolocutory function occurs in the satire is removed from the satirist by dialogue and adversary. The lecturer may be thought to speak for Catius, but not for Horace, who greets the report of his lecture with a mock deference clearly bespeaking skepticism.

If Stertinius and the unnamed Epicurean are twice removed from the satirist, Crispinus, in *Sat.* II. vii, is thrice removed. Davus, Horace's slave, reports, again in dialogue, a fellow servant's account of Crispinus' Stoic sermon on the paradox that only the wise are free. Although Crispinus is thus reported at third hand, he seems nevertheless, unlike Stertinius and the Epicurean, acceptable to Horace, who, though he growls at Davus for applying the sermon to him, seems disposed to tolerate as profitable this look at himself. As far as Horace is concerned, then, Crispinus functions like a second adversary, and it is only with Davus that he may be thought of as performing a prolocutory role.[8]

It is a little surprising that Horace, with his negligent temper, did not resort more often to the prolocutor than he did. It is more surprising that Juvenal, with his positive temper, resorted to it at all. But he did, in his *Third Satire*, which is very nearly a monologue by the prolocutor, with only the briefest introduction by the satirist. Why he had Umbricius speak for him is not far to seek of course. It would have been absurd, as Gilbert Highet remarks, "for a satirist to stay in Rome and recite a dozen reasons for leaving."[9] But it may also have occurred to Juvenal that the use of a prolocutor such as Umbricius, that is, a good man driven out of the city by his refusal to accommodate to its vices and perils, would be more effective witness to the evils of megalopolis than any diatribe delivered by the satirist himself. Also, a prolocutor in such a case affords the advantage of suggesting that the crimes complained of are quite real and that satirists are not the only ones conscious of them or incensed by them. Perhaps these reasons, as much as anything else, account for Juvenal's decision

8. It should be noted too that for Horace, apart from serving as vicarious adversary (edifier), Crispinus lends credibility to the spectacle of philosophy in the mouth of a slave. Something like this also explains why there is here a third party in the chain leading to the prolocutory character. Davus would hardly have been eligible to attend the lecture hall, just as Crispinus's own doorman could not, but had to overhear. It is credible enough, on the other hand, that Davus should have had the lecture from a fellow servant who himself got it by eavesdropping.

9. Gilbert Highet, *Juvenal the Satirist* (Oxford: Clarendon, 1954), p. 68.

to use honest Umbricius and to report him in direct discourse. Two prolocutors and three *discipuli*. Not a rich yield for the founders of satire. Perhaps this too, along with the fact that all but one belong to Horace, the least attractive to the Renaissance of the Roman satirists, explains the absence of prolocutory satire in English before Pope, and its singularity in his hands.[10]

The Second Satire of the Second Book of Horace Paraphrased appeared in mid–1734. Though Pope owed the idea to Horace, and certain obvious guidelines in the adaptation, he made the prolocutor his own from the outset and turned him to uses Horace had no occasion for, if notion of. One of the chief of these was the adjustment of the personal morality of the original toward a public (political) morality. Of this we shall have more to say later; for the moment we may look at the prolocutor himself.

Pope's Bethel, though a countryman (Yorkshire), was no farmer in the class of Ofellus, but rather a country gentleman,

10. The possibility that Pope experimented with epistolary adaptation of the prolocutor is suggested by certain tokens in the *Ethic Epistles*. Like Persius, he resorts to something resembling nonce usage in the opening of *To a Lady*, where he attributes to Martha Blount the unflattering observation about character in women. Less close is the opening of the *Epistle to Bathurst*, where, however, besides the epistolary variation, the speaker does not represent the satirist's point of view. In the *Burlington* there is a curious ambiguity, or hover, between prolocutor and epistolist beginning in v. 39 and continuing at least to about v. 71: "Oft have you hinted to your brother Peer,/A Certain truth, which many buy too dear:/Something there is more needful than Expence," etc. This skillfully creates the possibility of double reading: either as the words of the satirist or those of some acknowledged expert. The *Cobham* also opens with a hint of prolocutory usage, but it falls under the same disqualifications as the *Bathurst* and *To a Lady*.

In the *Sober Advice*, as in its original, there is a hover between prolocutory and monologic impression in the closing lines, where Pope makes it possible to read the plea for a "willing Nymph," the dubious tribute to *Montagu*, and the account of the surprised adulterer, as the utterance of Bathurst. The advantage in this case is obvious, the subject matter being such that it would have been reckless of Pope to broach it unequivocally *in propria persona*.

one acquainted with the simple life more from choice than from necessity or hard experience.[11] It is this fact which, in addition to Pope's desire to introduce himself, determined his dismissal at that point in the satire where Horace brought Ofellus to the fore. Though Bethel's station in life would not lend itself to such an account of his experience as Ofellus gives, Pope, though not so much a farmer as either, could find circumstances in his own life readily adaptable to the Ofellian posture.

The differences between Bethel and Ofellus are not such, however, as to disqualify the former for something like the rural decorum, and Pope imparts to him, even more consistently than Horace to Ofellus, the countryman's simplicity and brevity of speech. Compare, for example, Pope's version of Bethel's opening remarks with Horace's version of Ofellus's:

> Go work, hunt, exercise! (he thus began)
> Then scorn a homely dinner, if you can.

11. Bethel was a part-time and gentleman farmer. He usually spent only his summers on the farm, his winters in town. According to Pope, however, his heart was always in the country: "I have often wished I could see you there [Yorkshire], where I fancy you are most happy; for in Town you generally seem to think yourself not at home. . . ." (letter of 31 July 1738, *Corr.*, IV, 113). Bethel was apparently philosophical by nature and inclination. Pope styles him such in a letter of 1727 (*Corr.*, II, 437). Martha Blount, writing with Pope, testifies to his moral habit: "as the season draws near for that universall Temptation of all Women, the Town, I shall want you to preach to me for my own good. . . ." (8 October 1731: *Corr.*, III, 233). Sherburn, though on what authority he does not indicate, speaks of his "love of simple living and diet" (*Corr.*, III, 209, *n.* 2). One may infer as much of course, not only from the poem, but from a number of Pope's letters to Bethel alluding to matters of diet, e.g., those of 27 November 1739 and 18 February 1739–40. It is interesting, finally, to note that Pope was writing to Bethel on the theme of tenancy, as opposed to ownership, as early as 1726: "I am of old Ennius his mind, *Nemo me decoret lachrymis*—I am but a *Lodger* here: this is not an abiding City. I am only to stay out my lease, for what has Perpetuity and mortal man to do with each other? But I could be glad you would take up with an Inn at Twitenham, as long as I am Host of it. . . ." (*Corr.*, II, 387).

This telescopes some six and a half Horatian hexameters, hexameters which, moreover, admit as much of the poet as of the farmer:

. . . . leporem sectatus, equove
lassus ab indomito vel, etc.[12]

Similarly, "Your wine lock'd up" and *nisi Hymettia mella Falerno/ne biberis diluta;* "Or fish deny'd, (the River yet un-thaw'd)" and *et atrum/defendens piscis hiemat mare;* and

Preach as I please, I doubt our curious men
Will chuse a Pheasant still before a Hen.

Vix tamen eripiam, posito pavone velis quin
hoc potius quam gallina tergere palatum, etc.[13]

Since, whatever other reasons he may have had, Pope intended to substitute himself for Bethel in the conclusion of the poem, he took greater pains than Horace to create and sustain an illusion of style in his prolocutor.[14]

12. Vv. 9 ff. "After hunting the hare or being wearied by an unruly horse, or (if, accustomed to the Greek, the Roman exercise fatigues you), whether, out of excitement the swift ball pleasingly lightens the strenuous exercise, or the discus (hurl the discus through the yielding air)—when exercise has worked off squeamishness, dry and hungry, despise then (if you can) plain food."

13. Vv. 23–24. "Yet if a peacock were served up, I should hardly be able to prevent your gratifying the palate with it rather than a pullet." Ofellus is made much more elaborate in this speech, even as it continues, than Bethel. Cf. Bethel, vv. 61–66, Ofellus, vv. 63–69; Bethel, v. 69 ff., Ofellus, v. 71 ff.; Bethel, vv. 123–128, and Ofellus, vv. 106–111.

14. Professor Thomas Maresca, *Pope's Horatian Poems* (Columbus: The Ohio State University Press, 1966), pp. 214–221, is undoubtedly correct in seeing the Christian as well as lexical meaning of *sermon* operating in Pope's imitation, but I am less inclined to stress this aspect than he. What Professor Maresca sees in terms of pulpit decorum I see in terms of the rural decorum and Pope's desire and need to distinguish his prolocutor's style from his own. In connection with this rural decorum, there is an interesting, and so far as I know singular, piece of evidence where Bethel is concerned. It is in a fragment of a letter from Pope to Bethel, preserved in Ruffhead, but undatable:

This is not to say that Bethel's speech is simply rural in character. Pope applies to it, not only the artistically necessary selection of language really spoken by men, but also that variety which his prolocutor himself (the real Bethel) obliged him to apply. In Bethel's case, however, unlike that of Ofellus, the variation is more nearly witty than eloquent. In place of literary flourish, Bethel's sermon is seasoned with epigram, satiric vignette and epithet, play on words, and irony. Such embellishment is modest, however, and kept entirely consonant with the essentially forthright decorum of his discourse.

Though Bethel's prolocutory function is of course generally rhetorical, or persuasive, in design, it takes three particular aspects. Prudentially, Bethel serves Pope, as Ofellus may or may not have served Horace, as spokesman for a virtue—moderation in diet—which Pope evidently honored more in the breach than in the observance, and which he could not therefore safely proclaim *in propria persona*.[15] Dramatically, he serves to set the stage for Pope's re-entry at the end and to provide a kind of foil against which Pope could play his own personality, with all that this implies for the success of the poem. In this respect, Bethel makes possible, not only dramatic preparation and contrast, but climax as well. Thematically, Bethel is of course responsible for the lesson in moderation, but that is not the only, nor the central, theme of the poem, and Bethel functions further to provide a crucial link between the burden of *his* discourse and that of

---

I am so aukward at writing letters, to such as expect me to write like a wit, that I take any course to avoid it. 'Tis to you only, and a few such plain honest men, I like to open myself with the same freedom, and as free from all disguises, not only of sentiment, *but of style*, as they themselves. (*Corr.*, III, 519. Italics mine.)

15. Note Bathurst's observation on Pope's "intemperance" in diet (*Corr.*, III, 414, *n.* 1); also Dr. Cheyne's appelation, "Gluttonous Pretender . . . to Philosophy" (*Ibid.*, IV, 46). Kent called Pope "the greatest Glutton I know." (*Ibid.*, p. 150).

Pope's—property and its place in the human scheme and the human duty. By his allusion to politics, moreover, Bethel broadens the ethical application to include public as well as private virtue, and so implies the ultimate issue in Pope's adaptation— an issue which, though in part theologically argued, is not theological at all, but social, based on theological premises. As spokesman on this plane, Bethel is especially effective. He represents, in the satiric strategy, an impartial voice (no axe to grind), a voice uncompromised therefore by political distrust, and a voice which can be taken to reflect the traditional and abiding English virtues. In these respects he is rather more like Umbricius than Ofellus, a circumstance not particularly surprising when we consider the greater proximity of Juvenal's theme to Pope's. It is, at any rate, not enough for the satirist to have someone else initiate his political allusion; he needs it done by someone like Bethel: blameless, respected, unexceptionably English in character, sentiment, and habit.

It is not necessary to dwell on the prudential and dramatic functions of Bethel. Once attention is directed to them, they tend to explicate themselves. It may be worthwhile, though, to take brief notice of one special instance of the prudential function. Besides serving as stand-in for Pope on a theme he could not comfortably preach about in his own person, Bethel is made to pronounce a kind of absolution on the very disability which required his spokesmanship:

> On morning wings how active springs the Mind,
> That leaves the load of yesterday behind?
> How easy ev'ry labour it pursues?
> How coming to the Poet ev'ry Muse?
> Not but we may exceed, some Holy time,
> Or tir'd in search of Truth, or search of Rhyme.
> Ill Health some just indulgence may engage,
> And more, the Sickness of long life, Old-Age. [81–88]

Ofellus, who made the allowances originally, said nothing about poets, but Pope recognized himself, a little ruefully no doubt, and not a little gratefully, in the Roman's *tenuatum corpus*.

It is the political thrust of Bethel's sermon, however, that constitutes his subtlest and most significant office. Though it manifests itself early and proves ultimately pervasive, it is kept indicative in the sermon and its full enunciation is reserved for Pope. But it is important to Pope that Bethel should initiate the allusion.

Bethel begins, like Dr. Johnson, where he means to end, with a glance at the Court, as the symbol, if not the source, of luxury. He resorts, in this first instance, to the obliquity of peerage:

> Of *Carps* and *Mullets* why prefer the great,
> (Tho' cut in pieces e'er my Lord can eat).   [21–22]

What makes this suspicious—as something other than casual adaptation—is the absence in Horace of any suggestion of aristocratic association. Ofellus says simply, "You praise, O foolish fellow, a three-pound mullet, which you are obliged to cut into little pieces."[16] The same inference attaches, a little later, to Bethel's "Peer" (v. 40), substituted for Ofellus's *praetor* (v. 50).

Bethel turns next to partisanship as the vehicle of allusion. Where Ofellus says, "If any were to give out that roasted gulls are delicious, our Roman youth, readily taught in depravity, would acquiesce,"[17] Bethel gives the observation a political turn with a play on the word *party*:

> Let me extoll a *Cat* on Oysters fed,
> I'll have a Party at the Bedford Head.   [41–42]

16. Vv. 33–34: laudas, insane, trilibrem/mullum, in singula quem minuas pulmenta necesse est.

17. Vv. 51–52: si quis nunc mergos suavis edixerit assos,/parebit pravi docilis Romana iuventus.

Then, abandoning indirection, he brings the allusion squarely to target:

> Or ev'n to crack live *Crawfish* recommend,
> I'd never doubt at Court to make a Friend.   [43-44]

From here on there can be little doubt as to the prolocutor's drift.

The adaptation of Avidienus was no doubt prompted by the motive that always brought the Wortley Montagus onto Pope's satiric page, but their affiliation with the Court makes political allusion an added certainty. As nearly always in Pope, too, if Lady Mary appear, Lord Hervey cannot be far behind, in this case as Bethel's nominee for an undenominated role in Horace (vv. 94-95). The terms of his indictment are worth pausing over, for they signify the destiny of private virtue in public virtue which is the ultimate point of the imitation:

> Unworthy He, the voice of Fame to hear,
> (That sweetest Music to an honest ear;
> For 'faith Lord Fanny: you are in the wrong,
> The World's good word is better than a Song)
> Who has not learn'd, fresh Sturgeon and Ham-pye
> Are no rewards for Want, and Infamy!   [99-104]

As for Avidien and his wife, they are made to represent the meanness of Courtly example, as Lord Fanny and the other Lordships of the poem represent its extravagance and luxury.

Bethel's political allusion is not confined to the Court, however, but ranges from that high place to its symptomatic reflection on the lower levels of clerical and oppidan life and to its anticipation in the mercenary standard of Marlborough. Thus the clerico-municipal turn given the Horatian *cena dubia*:

> How pale, each Worshipful and rev'rend Guest
> Rise from a Clergy, or a City, feast!
> What life in all that ample Body, say,

What heav'nly Particle inspires the clay?
The Soul subsides; and wickedly inclines
To seem but mortal, ev'n in sound Divines.   [75-80]

The passage which Marlborough's name concludes and which
"his Lordship" introduces, defines the misuse of riches in terms
unmistakably public and by implication political:

"Right, cries his Lordship, for a Rogue in need
"To have a Taste, is Insolence indeed:
"In me 'tis noble, suits my birth and state
"My wealth unwieldy, and my heap too great."
Then, like the Sun, let Bounty spread her ray,
And shine that Superfluity away.
Oh Impudence of wealth! with all thy store,
How dar'st thou let one worthy man be poor?
Shall half the new-built Churches round thee fall?
Make Keys, build Bridges, or repair White-hall:
Or to thy Country let that heap be lent,
As M**o's was, but not at five *per Cent*.   [111-122]

Here, as elsewhere, the prolocutor is arguing in effect "the
private in the public good," that not only "Self-love and Social,"
but Self-wrong and Social, are the same.

It is possible, indeed, that Bethel's allusion reaches, by a most
circumspect approach, as high as the King himself. We know
that his references to better times are implicitly political; what is
not so apparent is that they may be tacitly royal as well. When,
for example, he says,

Cheap eggs, and herbs, and olives still we see,
Thus much is left of old Simplicity!   [35-36]

he omits from his original what its facing text still afforded the
reader, namely, *epulis regum*: "Nor is the pauper's fare yet
wholly banished from *the feasts of kings*" (43-44). Similarly,
when he complains,

> Why had not I in those good times my birth,
> E're Coxcomb-pyes or Coxcombs were on earth?   [97–98]

he again departs from the original in such a way as to direct
attention to its facing text:

> . . . . hos utinam inter
> heroas natum tellus me prima tulisset!   [92–93]

"Oh that the primal world had granted me birth among such
heroes as those [*antiqui* = Pope's "Our Fathers"]." That this is a
mode of allusion-by-omission to George's heroic pretensions
gains probability from what looks like a recurrence of it in the
concluding lines of Bethel's sermon:

> And who stands safest, tell me? is it he
> That spreads and swells in puff'd Prosperity,
> Or blest with little, whose preventing care
> In Peace provides fit arms against a War? [18]

By itself this looks innocent enough: a moral admonition. But on
the facing page one reads this:

> O magnus posthac inimicis risus! uterne
> ad casus dubios fidet sibi certius? hic qui
> pluribus adsuerit mentem corpusque superbum,
> an qui contentus parvo metuensque futuri
> in pace, ut sapiens, aptarit idonea bello?   [107–111]

"Oh, you, who shall hereafter be the laughing-stock of your
enemies, which of the two shall count upon himself in vicissi-
tude with more certainty—he who has served his mind and body
to redundancy, or he who, content with little and mindful of the
future, has in peace, like a wise man, readied himself for war?"
Sober advice for a monarch vain of military glory, frustrated by a
peace policy which made him the laughing stock of enemies
abroad, and driven by a carnal alliance which made him a
scandal at home:

18. Vv. 125–128. See also below, p. 44 ff.

What seas [he] travers'd! and what fields [he]
    fought!
[His] Country's Peace, how oft, how dearly bought!

Looking back at Bethel's sermon, what seemed at first simply a
discourse on personal morality proves at last a discourse on
public morality, with special reference to Courtly example.
Hardly an article in Bethel's creed does not make its point by
reference to public life, particularly in its political aspect. This is
precisely where Pope wants to carry the argument for morality,
and in broaching it the prolocutor has made it seem not only
inescapable but just and impartial.

When Pope takes over from Bethel, at that point where
Horace receded in favor of Ofellus, he modulates the theme of
temperance to the more inclusive one of *dominium,* a transition
implicit all along in Bethel's sermon but plainly adumbrated in
its concluding lines. But the real carryover is achieved on the
level of the political allusion, which Bethel initiated as the
symbol of luxury and miserliness in the public life and which
Pope enhances now as the symbol of failure to distinguish
between the claims of property (*dominium*) and of stewardship
(*usufructus*). On this theme, unlike that of temperance, Pope
can afford to speak out in his own person. The result is an
orchestration, so to speak, of two distinct but related themes, of
the political allusion which links them both on the public level,
and of the voice and personality of the poet, who gives wings to
the sober advice of Bethel.[19]

The whole orchestral effect is stated at once in Pope's adaptation of Horace's observation (vv. 113–14) about Ofellus's stead-
fastness in the face of changing fortune. Pope adapts this to
himself in such a way as to suggest, by its antithetical and

---

19. Cf. Pope's own distinction: "Thus said our Friend, and what he *said* I
sing." (V. 68, italics mine.)

allusive formulation, a complex tissue of sense and symbol: the interdependence of public and private morality, the fall from a state of public virtue to a state of public vice, and the private virtue as the saving remnant in such a crisis. Thus:

> In *South-sea* days not happier, when surmis'd
> The Lord of thousands, than if now *Excis'd;*
> In Forest planted by a Father's hand,
> Than in five acres now of rented land.   [133–136]

At least three levels of allusion collaborate here: personal, Scriptural, and historical (political). The first is to the satirist's own past and present and to his moral resolution in the face of the difference to him. The second, disclosed specifically in such tokens as *lord, forest, father,* and the *exile* phonetically and semantically latent in *excise,* is Edenic and lapsarian. The last closes the circle, juxtaposing the Harleian promise of prosperity and the Walpollian threat of impoverishment, the pastoral amplitude of Queen Anne Windsor and the rent-rate circumference of Hanoverian Twickenham. All three illuminate the point, first broached in the political reflex of Bethel's speech, that private morality is ultimately a matter of public performance, and that the two are in fact inseparable.

The same tendency to bend the significance outward, to assert the public responsibility of private morality, marks Pope's adaptation of Ofellus's account of his simple hospitality (vv. 118 ff.):

> But ancient friends, (tho' poor, or out of play)
> That touch my Bell, I cannot turn away.   [139–140]

The gambling metaphor is a palpable glance at Tory and Patriot "outs," and the couplet containing it must have taken on added significance for Pope after mid–1733, when Whigs of the Opposition, friends like Chesterfield and Cobham, along with others, were summarily dismissed from office and honors for their opposition to the Excise. But Pope's point is thematic as well as personal, and the verses afford another image of private virtue in remonstrance with public vice (neglect, ingratitude, and the like).

We have remarked earlier, in discussing Bethel's prolocutory role, the likelihood of Pope's reliance upon the facing text of Horace to speak to his purposes by its testimony to his omissions as well as adaptations. That Pope viewed the whole question of *dominium* in this poem as primarily political (social) and only secondarily (supportively) theological in significance, can be inferred from another such testimony of his facing text: the omissions from Ofellus's remarks about his new landlord, best quoted in this instance from that text, by reason of its italics.

> . . . . quanto aut *ego* parcius, aut *vos*
> O pueri nituistis, ut huc *novus Incola* venit?
> Nam *propriæ telluris* herum natura neque illum
> Nec me, aut quemquam statuit; nos expulit ille,
> Illum aut *Nequities*, aut *vafri inscitia juris*,
> Postremo expellit certe *vivacior hæres*.[20]

Part of this Pope renders in this place:

> Tho' double-tax'd, how little have I lost?
> My Life's amusements have been just the same,
> Before, and after Standing Armies came.
> My lands are sold, my father's house is gone;
> I'll hire another's, is not that my own,
> And yours my friends? . . .   [152–157]

---

20. Vv. 107–112 in the numbering of the Twickenham facing text. I have normalized the italic style and supplied terminal punctuation. The passage translates, "How much more sparing *I*, or less blooming *you*, my lads, since this new *landlord* came. Nature makes nor him, nor me, nor any, *lord of this land*. He drove us out; him either *iniquity* or *ignorance of the subtleties of the law*, or, at least, an *heir of longer life* shall expell."

More of it he will render later, in his lines on property (167–178). What he says here alludes of course to the Catholic penal laws and to the Opposition quarrel with standing armies. So much has he adapted from Horace. But just as significant, if not more so, is what he has left untouched: Ofellus's references to a new landlord (*Incola* = foreign resident),[21] his usurpation (*nos expulit ille*), the villainy around him, and his ignorance (*Nequities . . . vafri inscitia juris*), and the heir likely to outlive him (*vivacior hæres*). It is impossible to believe that Pope did not perceive the perfect aptness of these lines and that he would not expect his reader to notice their omission in the imitation. They frame a devastating allusion to George II, Hanoverian England, and the perversion of *dominium*. Their omission is eloquent and almost certainly calculated.

That such an inference is not gratuitous is further argued by the palpable allusion of the concluding couplet of the poem:

> Let Lands and Houses have what Lords they will,
> Let Us be fix'd, and our own Masters still.

Here, in the classic style of his ambiguous mode, Pope speaks at once of acreage, residences, and property owners; and of countries, dynasties, and princes—England, the House of Hanover, and George.

Neither is it fanciful to see the political allusion sustained in the glances at the venal and other mercenary uses of property in the closing lines of the poem, the references to Peter Walter,[22] "a

21. *Landlord* translates *incola*, which is literally *inhabitant* or *resident*, but which can also mean, by extension, *immigrant, foreign resident*. Pope would certainly have seen the latter meaning as suggestive of the Hanoverian posture, and would have counted on his reader to do the same.

22. Cf. Swift's description of Walters in *To Mr. Gay on his being Steward to the Duke of Queensberry* (1731): "Have *Peter Waters* always in your Mind;/That Rogue of *genuine ministerial* Kind:/Can half the Peerage by his Arts bewitch;/Starve twenty Lords to make one Scoundrel rich/ . . ." (*The Poems of Jonathan Swift*, ed. Harold Williams [Oxford: Clarendon, 1958], II, 534–535).

booby Lord," and the "City Knight." As for the poet—Pope—we have already observed how he presents himself in terms at once personal and public. We have come to expect of him that he would picture himself and his friends as patriots, seeking and finding consolation in retirement. But he seeks to impress us here particularly with the public conscience appropriate to the good man, with the public context in which he must inevitably transact the good life, with the public destiny of all things of this life and this world, and hence with the importance of a resolute virtue in the face of default in public office.

If we seem to have lost sight of Bethel and the prolocutor, that is as it should be—an effect of the role: to speak where the satirist could not; to provide an impartial and qualified witness to the failure of temperance in the land; to point allusively to Courtly and Ministerial responsibility; and then to step aside so that Pope could enlarge the thematic scope and claim the whole in behalf of satire and the satirist.

3

Sober Advice from Horace

$\mathbb{S}$OBER *Advice from Horace* has never fared well, and the reason, one suspects, is as much related to a failure to perceive its relevance as to any indecency, real or fancied, that is associated with it. Why, in his fit of imitating Horace, did Pope pitch upon this particular specimen, not especially reputable in the Horatian canon, and subject to dogged misgivings on the part of the Popeian constituency, including, apparently, even Pope himself? I shall suggest that he did so from motives neither perverse nor playful, as generally supposed, but rather ethical and satirical, in keeping with his recently assumed role of moral poet and imitator of Horace. Such a view will point, in turn, to the appropriateness of a reappraisal of the poem *qua* poem, the influences affecting its style and method, and the quality of its wit.[1]

1. *Sober Advice* has been treated variously as an "exercise in playful ribaldry" (R. K. Root, *Poetical Career of Alexander Pope,* p. 240*n*), a "somewhat libidinous" stratagem to enhance the reception of the *Arbuthnot* (Rogers, p. 71), "gloriously comic" in its description of bashful Jenny, but embarrassingly equivocal in its authorial duplicity (G. Tillotson, *Pope and Human Nature,* pp. 117, 222–23), a "fairly nasty imitation" of Horace's original, "insinuating and, in the notes if not in the text, pornographic" (R. Brower, *Alexander Pope,* p. 293), "racy," exploring "the perversity of cultivated lust," but not to "be taken very solemnly" (T. R. Edwards Jr., *This Dark Estate,* p. 84; see also pp. 100–101), and (most recently) "a quickly written *jeu d'esprit,* in which he [Pope] could blissfully forget about his

Sober Advice appeared anonymously in late 1734, "from the house of a hitherto untried bookseller."[2] It was never quite acknowledged by Pope, though it did appear in the Octavo edition of his *Works* in 1738, where it was retitled *The Second Satire of the First Book of Horace,* still "Imitated in the Manner of Mr. Pope."[3] It was then reprinted, unchanged, in the reissues of this edition in 1740 and 1743, but was omitted in the editions of Warburton (1751) and of Elwin-Courthope (1871–89). It has only recently been restored to the editorial canon by the Twickenham editor.

Pope is commonly supposed to have begun work on the poem at least by mid-year of 1734, though it is possible that its composition dates earlier than that.[4] That he had completed a draft of

---

painfully created public persona in order to amuse himself, his close friends, and his readers" (Leonard Moskovit, "Pope's Purposes in *Sober Advice," PQ,* XLIV [1965], p. 199).

2. See Griffith, I, 253 (headnote) and entry No. 347, pp. 262–263. The publication date was 28 December, the publisher was T. Boreman, and the poem was offered as "Imitated in the Manner of Mr. Pope." In 1738 T. Cooper reissued it under the title "A Sermon against Adultery: Being Sober Advice from Horace . . ." (Griffith, No. 489).

3. See Griffith, No. 507.

4. Mid–1734 is Sherburn's dating, from Bolingbroke's letter to Swift 27 June of that year. See *Corr.,* III, 413 and *n.* 3; 424, *n.* 2. It is tempting, however, to associate the composition with an earlier date, 20 March 1732–33, when Pope wrote to Caryll, "I've done another of Horace's Satires since I wrote to you last, and much in the same space of time as I did the former [i.e., *Sat.* II. i] . . ." Sherburn (*Corr.,* III, 358, *n.* 5) regards this new satire as Horace II. ii ("What, and how great, the Virtue and the Art"), though Butt (p. xxiv), who also takes mid–1734 as the composition date of *S.A.,* says, "It would be difficult to say which *Imitation* Pope was referring to; not to [*Sat.* II. ii], one must suppose, for to this he refers unmistakably as a poem just completed in a letter to Swift dated April 2, 1733, 'this week, *exercitandi gratia,* I have translated, or rather parodied, another of Horace's, in which I introduce you advising me about my expenses, housekeeping, &c.' " This letter, which Sherburn dates 20 April (*Corr.,* III, 365), he supposes simply mistakes the matter, and maintains that Pope is referring to the poem announced in the letter to Caryll, i.e., *Sat.* II. ii (*Corr.,* III, 336, *n.* 6). But there is clearly room for doubt, and nothing in the evidence precludes the

it by 27 June 1734 is evident from Bolingbroke's letter to Swift so dated. Pope has, says Bolingbroke,

been imitating the Satire of Horace which begins Ambubaiarum Collegia, Pharmacopolae, &c. and has chose rather to weaken the images than to hurt chaste ears overmuch. he has sent it to me, but I shall keep his secret, as he desires. . . .[5]

It was during August, at Lord Peterborow's, that, according to Sherburn, Pope "polished" *Sober Advice* while also putting together the *Epistle to Dr. Arbuthnot.*[6]

On 30 December, barely after its publication, Pope began the series of equivocal disclaimers of the poem which he had already anticipated by its anonymous and ambiguous title-page announcement. He writes to the Earl of Oxford, "I am Lord Duplin's humble Servant. I hope he will defend me from the imputation which all the Town I hear lay upon me, of having writ that impudent satire." The next day (31 December) he is protesting to Caryll:

Here is a piece of poetry from Horace come out, which I warn you not to take for mine, tho' some people are willing to fix it on me. In truth I should think it a very indecent Sermon, after the *Essay on Man.*

On 8 February 1734–35 he is still protesting to Caryll:

The ludicrous (or if you please) the obscene thing you desired me to send, I did not approve of, and therefore did not care to propagate by sending into the country at all. Whoever

---

possibility that, in the letter to Caryll, Pope was referring to *Sober Advice.* The earlier dating of *S.A.* would not only put it closer to the composition of *To a Lady,* to which it bears interesting resemblances, but also to Bentley's *Paradise Lost* (1732), his announced intention of doing an edition of Homer, and his second trial at Ely House, which was over by April 1734 (see R. C. Jebb, *Bentley,* [New York: Harper, 1902] pp. 115, 145).

5. *Corr.,* III, 413–414.
6. *Ibid.,* p. 424*n.*

likes it so well as to think it mine, compliments me at my own expense.

Something less than a fortnight later (18 February) he explains to Caryll the reaction of Bentley's son, word of which had apparently gotten around:

The story of Bentley is this in three words. He expressed a resentment as if I had injured his father in a thing I disowned. I told him if he was not satisfied in that, and if he required any other satisfaction, I would give it. After a three-weeks' hesitation, and messages, he gave it under his hand he did not, and confessed himself in the wrong.[7]

Why all this subterfuge and equivocation, and how is it to be judged? Sherburn interprets the matter bluntly: "Pope concealed his authorship because of the indecency of the poem and the threats of Bentley's son to horsewhip the poet, if he was the author."[8] Professor Rogers is more inventive:

Various features of this work as published were calculated to suggest that it was not Pope's composition but a parody of his style. The title page told readers that the poem had imitated Horace "in the Manner of Mr. Pope"; the imprint, "Printed for T. Boreman . . ." implied that the poem was the work of a Grub-street author. The general impression that such details create is that *Sober Advice* is an attack upon the satirist, an obscene parody of his manner in the *Imitations of Horace*. Pope evidently hoped that if readers could be made to think that *Sober Advice* was an abusive lampoon, they would be prepared to accept his apologia [the *Arbuthnot*] without question.[9]

---

7. For the quotations from the letters, see *ibid.*, pp. 446, 447, 450, 451. It is instructive to notice, by the way, the terms Pope applies to the composition as over against his equivocations about it. He calls it a *satire* (not, as Mr. Moskovit has termed it, a "libel"), a piece of *poetry*, a *sermon* (perhaps punningly), and *ludicrous* (it is "obscene" only "if you please").

8. *Corr.*, III, 446n.

9. Rogers, p. 71.

This theory, ingenious as it is (it is the *Dunciad* "ground bait" theory reapplied), is unsatisfactory on several counts. For one thing, it ignores the likelihood that if such were indeed Pope's motive, he missed a good opportunity to give it currency by suggesting it to Caryll, or, for that matter, to the Earl of Oxford. For another, it overlooks, as nearly everyone does, the testimony of Bolingbroke, who not only gives no indication of being aware of any such stratagem (only that Pope wished his authorship to remain unknown), but who seems to feel, moreover, that, far from being obscene, the poet has been rather scrupulous in rendering Horace. But even without these objections, it would not follow that because the poem is presented as parodic it was to be understood as obscene and abusive, that is, as damaging to Pope. That Pope himself feared the imputation of obscenity is something quite distinct from the supposition that the form of the poem and its manner of publication were calculated to provoke such a charge. The earlier *Imitations*, after all, were hardly innocent of lampoon, nor Pope himself of satiric obscenity, from the *Rape of the Lock* through the *Dunciad*, to the authorship of which he would own up in the very *apologia* that Rogers sees him preparing for in the indecency of *Sober Advice*. Nor is it easy to believe that Pope could (or would) have seriously entertained the idea that his title page would really persuade anybody that the poem which followed it was of Grubbaean origin:

> Poor guiltless I! and can I chuse but smile,
> When ev'ry Coxcomb knows me by my *Style*?

Pope, we must recognize, is as much in earnest as in jest here, and it is at some such point as this that the ultimate objection to Rogers must be made, for to accept his theory is to discredit the poem out of hand, to regard it *prima facie* as subpoetic, without sufficient wit or style to protect it from false attribution—conclusions that an unprejudiced reading of the poem will not, I believe, support. It seems more reasonable—and less costly—to assume that Pope's concern is not to fob the poem off on another, but to get it admitted to his own canon with as little embarrassment as possible.

As for the "indecency" of the poem, there both is and is not a question. At no point in its history has satire been distinguished for decency of manner, and the age and page of Pope are no exception. By the same token, at no point in its history has satire been exempt from complaint on that score, though the outcry has been perhaps the keener since the advent of sensibility. But indecency, as we know, is at least partly relative to time, place, and genre.[10] In Pope's case, moreover, it is relative to a hostility bred as much by his success (and politics) as by his satire; and, in the particular case in hand, by a new role he was striving at this point in his career to create for himself. In the process of building a reputation as a moral and philosophical poet, Pope had somehow to accommodate his genius to that end. Such accommodation is, of course, the problem of every satiric poet who is, at the same time, a serious (ethical) poet, but whose means (genius) is suspect. Hence the *apologia*. Hence too no doubt the recourse to epistolary and dialogic forms. Hence even, as Rogers suggests, the imitation itself.[11] Hence, finally, anonymity. However exalted his intent, the satirist's genius is satiric (and to that extent indecorous), and he must mediate these factors—ethics and satire—in the face of a stubborn reluctance on the part of the world to view them as compatible. The task is difficult, and the satirist rarely succeeds except in retrospect, and not always then.

This, at any rate, is something like the predicament of Pope at the time of turning to Horace's plain-spoken sermon on adultery.

10. For an impressive recent demonstration of this fact, see Alvin Kernan, *The Cankered Muse* (New Haven: Yale University Press, 1959).

11. Rogers, p. 78.

He is intent upon dignifying his profession as satirist, and he must take pains to avoid any misunderstanding, intentional or otherwise, that would compromise that aim. That Horace's poem is in fact, as I believe Pope recognized, entirely consonant with his moral and philosophical program, could have afforded little consolation, for Pope was experienced enough to know that not many would be so sophisticated as to realize it, or so candid as to acknowledge it if they did. Just, therefore, as he earlier published the *Essay on Man* anonymously, while at the same time publishing other pieces under his name, in order to outwit his critics and gain an unprejudiced hearing for his venture into dogmatic poetry, so in *Sober Advice* he may be thought of as resorting to a similar strategy in behalf of another radical venture. Pope's whole career was a composition of just such defensive tactics relative to the expression of his genius, and there is no reason to suppose that (save for his Catholic friends, whom he always tried to spare) he donned the cloak of anonymity in this particular instance for any reason other than a lack of confidence in the candor of his audience. His adaptation is licentious, to be sure, but so is its model. That is implicit in their nature, as satires. It is, as Pope knew, no necessary Friend of Virtue who protests,

> This filthy Simile, this beastly Line,
> Quite turns my Stomach—

and thus he rejoins,

> So does Flatt'ry mine;
> And all your Courtly Civet-Cats can vent,
> Perfume to you, to me is Excrement.

Sober Advice is not gross, or nasty, but witty and, in the best (satiric) sense of the word, shocking. But Pope could not count upon the world knowing or acknowledging the difference.

Hence—and not in some tacit confession of guilt or shame—the anonymity of its publication.[12]

A fair summation of the matter would, then, seem to be this: that Pope indeed published *Sober Advice* anonymously because he was accustomed to proceeding in this fashion whenever he sensed danger, either to his reputation or to his person; but that he also resorted to anonymity because he wanted to venture his newly assumed profession of moral poetry in a genre, model, and tone he could not be certain would take, and so divested the experiment of such disadvantages as his name would almost certainly visit upon it. It is this last motive in fact which defines my basic proposition regarding the poem, that far from being an indecent excursion into the "pornographic," or even something

12. Judged by the standards of satire, including that of the eighteenth century, and by comparison with Horace himself, Bolingbroke was more nearly right about Pope's "decency" than the complainants on that score. Beside *est qui/Inguen ad obscaenum subductis usque facetus* (vv. 25–26) bashful Jenny with her "Fore-Buttocks," which have scandalized many, though they pleased Tillotson, seems decent enough. Pope will retain, as his age was wont, Horace's *perminxerunt* (Horace, 44; Pope, 56), but he tones down *Accidit, ut cuidam* TESTIS, CAUDAMQUE SALACEM . . ." (45) to "One bleeds in Person" (58). He has Horatian authority (*mutonis*) for "that honest Part that rules us all" (87), and he renders *cunnum* by the popular and yet decently ambiguous term "Thing." His "rise" (88), latent in the idea of *muto*, gains additional support from Horace's *mea cum conferbuit ira* (also rendered, later, by "Or when my pulse beat highest," v. 91). The embellishment of Horace's *Quid responderet? Magno patre nata puella est* (72)—put in terms of venereal embarrassment—is characteristically witty, not smutty: "What would you answer? Could you have the Face,/When the poor Suff'rer humbly mourn'd his Case,/To cry 'You weep the Favours of her GRACE?" (93–95). In the passage which follows (96–105) he elaborates Horace's "moral" and ventures another metaphor for *muto*—"God's good Thing." Horace's *dum futuo* (127) is given the perfectly decent expression "in the Fact." We shall have further occasion, in the text, to see how Pope translates Horace's blunt Latin into witty periphrasis. As for the Bentleyan footnotes, Professor Moskovit has admirably met the objection that these are pornographic. By the token of the *persona* there represented, these notes, as he shows (pp. 198–199), belong not to Pope, but to the pedant, to whom they are altogether appropriate.

so innocent as "a quickly written *jeu d'esprit,*" *Sober Advice* is in reality an exercise in a different key in the very moral and philosophic scheme Pope had undertaken with the *Essay on Man* and *Ethic Epistles.*

It is not necessary to rehearse the grand, complex, and shifting design of that ambitious undertaking. Pope expressed the essence of it in "The Design" prefixed to *An Essay on Man:*

> Having proposed to write some pieces on Human Life and Manners, such as (to use my lord Bacon's expression) *come home to Men's Business and Bosoms,* I thought it more satisfactory to begin with considering *Man* in the abstract.
>
> .   .   .   .
>
> What is now published, is only to be considered as a *general Map* of MAN . . . leaving the particular to be more fully delineated in the charts which are to follow. Consequently, these Epistles in their progress . . . will be less dry, and more susceptible of poetical ornament.[13]

Pope was anxious from the outset not to lose the poet in the philosopher, nor, as his performance makes clear, the satirist in the poet. Even the *Essay,* though it "stands apart from the satires . . . [has] an obvious satiric flavor,"[14] and this flavor becomes more pronounced in the *Ethic Epistles,* which are generally acknowledged to be essentially Horatian satires. Pope was, in short, in a Horatian mood of teaching and speaking, and was expressing that mood in the following sequence of publications:

Epistle to Burlington [Ethic Epistle IV], December 1731
Epistle to Bathurst [Ethic Epistle III], January
    1733 N. S.
Imitation of Horace [*Sat.* II. i], February 1733 N. S.
An Essay on Man [Epistles I–III], February–May 1732–33

13. *An Essay on Man* (Twickenham, ed. Maynard Mack), pp. 7–8.
14. Rogers, p. 52. Brower (p. 207 ff.) remarks the poem's affinity with the "Horatian diatribe-epistle."

Epistle to Cobham [Ethic Epistle I], January 1734 N. S.
An Essay on Man [Epistle IV], January 1734 N. S.
Imitation of Horace [*Sat.* II. ii], July 1734
Sober Advice from Horace [*Sat.* I. ii], December 1734
Epistle to Dr. Arbuthnot, January 1735 N. S.
To a Lady [Ethic Epistle II], February 1735 N. S.
    Etc.

Sober Advice, which gives back echo stronger or fainter to every piece in the list, conforms to Pope's general purpose in the series ("some pieces on Human Life and Manners") and bears a particular affinity to the *Epistle to Cobham* ("Of the Knowledge and Characters of Men") and to the *Epistle to a Lady* ("Of the Characters of Women"). *To a Lady* was composed by January 1733 N. S., but not published until February 1735 N. S. *Cobham* was composed, or was in composition, apparently between April and October or November 1733 and published the following January.[15] Depending on how one looks at the question of the composition date of *Sober Advice,* the order of composition of the three pieces would be either

To a Lady: by Jan. 1733 N. S.	⎫ ⎧ *To a Lady*
Cobham: April to Oct.–Nov. 1733	⎬ or ⎨ *S. A.:* 20 March 1733 N. S.
Sober Advice: by 27 June 1734	⎭ ⎩ *Cobham*

After *To a Lady,* or perhaps concurrently with its composition, Pope turned to Horace: *Satire* II. i, composed December–January 1732–33 and *Satire* II. ii, composed before the end of March 1733. He then turned either to the *Cobham,* as commonly supposed, or, as it may be—out of the momentum generated by *Satires* II. i and ii—to *Sober Advice* (I. ii). But in any case, *Sober Advice* comes either between or on the heels of *To a Lady* and *Cobham.* When, in other words, Pope turned to *Ambubaiarum collegia,* he was in the midst of his program of

15. See Rogers, pp. 38–39.

discourse on "Human Life and Manners" in "the Horatian way," and was more proximately engaged in studies of the "Characters" of men and women, both of which are at issue in Horace's satire and Pope's adaptation of it. What more consistent, given the Horatian reflex and the start on the *sermones,* than to turn at such a juncture to *Satire* I. ii? No other of the satires could have served Pope's purposes as well.

Though not very like *Sober Advice* in style and technique, *Cobham* is thematically close to the Imitation. It begins by acknowledging the baffling inconsistency in the characters of men, the inconsistency that leads one to this extreme, another to that, and the same man now to one extreme, now to another. This is the very point of Horace's complaint in *Sat.* I. ii, which he expresses *Dum vitant stulti vitia, in contraria currunt,* and which Pope renders, highlighting the sexual duality, "Women and Fools are always in extreme."[16] But the ultimate burden of *Cobham,* as more or less of the other parts of the *magnum opus,* is the idea of the Ruling Passion, which biases a man in some peculiar direction. *Sober Advice* addresses itself, on a more satirical level, to one of the commonest of such biases, the adulterous or venerean passion. To the folly of that passion, Horace, and with him Pope, brings a commonsense cure, of course, but beneath the urbanity of the one and the audacity of the other lies a common indictment of the expense of spirit in a waste of shame. Finally, though its scope extends beyond any single passion, *Cobham* amply alludes to the adulterous and venerean passions and persons with which and whom *Sober Advice* deals exclusively. Besides its mistresses (vv. 55–56), punks (83–84, 190–91), and whores (212–213), *Cobham* affords the following sobering spectacle:

16. This line and its idea are very nearly repeated in *To a Lady,* v. 113: "Woman and Fool are two hard things to hit." The basic formula recurs in *Cobham* (v. 183): "Women and Fools must like him or he dies." This repetition constitutes another argument for the kinship of these poems.

Behold a rev'rend sire, whom want of grace
Has made the father of a nameless race,
Shov'd from the wall perhaps, or rudely press'd
By his own son, that passes by unbless'd:
Still to his wench he crawls on knocking knees,
And envies ev'ry sparrow that he sees.

[vv. 228–233]

To a Lady verges even closer on *Sober Advice,* partly by
virtue of its greater satiric particularity, partly by virtue of its
concern with women, but chiefly by virtue of its basic device, the
gallery of satiric portraits, the latter of which almost certainly
influenced the opening of the Horatian imitation, affecting the
sex and manner of Pope's adaptation, with its parade of Old-
fields, Fufidias, Rufas, and the like.[17] As Bentley is made to
complain in the footnotes, the corresponding characters in Horace are male. Though Pope turns to the male soon enough (v.
35 ff.), he commences the Imitation in the spirit and manner of
To a Lady. The influence, as it turns out, is a happy one,
consistent with the different times, habits, and vision of the
English satirist. By it Pope was able to update Horace to the
eighteenth-century taste for satire on women, to achieve a
greater initial energy and impact than his original, and, most
significantly, to bring to the forefront of the satire the object of
the folly that it decries and ridicules.

Among the ladies in this later, less glamorous gallery, *Rufa*
had appeared, by name at least, in the earlier, where (vv.
21–23), though no whore, she is perhaps but a coquette's remove therefrom. Oldfield appears in the *Cobham* (vv.
242–247), and Fufidia (under her more common sobriquet,
Sappho) in *To a Lady,* where she is no more wholesome than

---

17. It should be remarked, however, that in respect of status some of Pope's
women in *Sober Advice* may hark from an inspiration different from those of
To a Lady. One suspects that Moll (and Jack), Peg and Jenny derive from
the lower world of Swift's burlesque and lampoon.

here, though for different reasons. Peg and bashful Jenny, though they have no counterpart in the Epistle, qualify, in their fashion, for the role assigned to Narcissa there:

> A very Heathen in the carnal part,
> Yet still a sad, good Christian at her heart.

Like the *Cobham, To a Lady* also takes ample notice of the adulterous and venerean passions. We catch a fleeting glimpse of them in Leda and Magdalen, and we have already remarked Narcissa's weaknesses that way. In addition there is *Philomedé*, "Proud as a Peeress, prouder as a Punk"; she "whose life the Church and Scandal share"; and *Chloe*, with her "Lover [panting] upon her breast." Every woman, as Pope observes, "is at heart a Rake."

> You purchase Pain with all that Joy can give,
> And die of nothing but a rage to live.   [99–100]

> For foreign glory, foreign joy, they roam;
> No thought of Peace or Happiness at home.   [223–224]

> A Fop their Passion, but their Prize a Sot,
> Alive, ridiculous, and dead, forgot!   [247–248]

To these observations on the folly of womankind may be compared similar sentiments on that of mankind in *Sober Advice*, especially verses 77–80, 96–101, and 143–146. It is as if after he had done *To a Lady* Pope recalled in Horace the ideal counterpart, "To a Man."[18] The parallels, at any rate, are striking, and suggest a certain continuity in design as well as theme. Pope has not shifted ground in *Sober Advice*, but intensified what he was already about, thematically in general and procedurally in aspects of *To a Lady*.

It will be appropriate now to reopen the question of the art of *Sober Advice*, as much misjudged, I believe, as its motives. Since

18. He addressed *Sober Advice* "To the Young Gentlemen about Town."

the poem is an imitation, this question may best be approached from that standpoint, that is, of what Pope did with his original. As usual, he follows his model fairly closely in substance and arrangement, but executes those local variations that make the difference between translation and imitation.[19] In this instance, apart from what we have already remarked about the influence of *To a Lady*, the variations will be found to be chiefly, though not exclusively, a tissue of high lampoon and *double-entendre*. Pope, as always, intensifies Horace: particularizes his reference and sharpens his edge, scandalizes his nose for satire, converts his Latin into racy English, and draws him masterfully into those orbits of wit so congenial to his own age and genius: the comedy and conscience of the Restoration, Swift and the burlesque vein, and the happy malice and audacity of Mr. Pope himself. But he saw his imitative art precisely in proportion to these innovations on his original, and he cannot be judged except as they are taken into account.[20]

19. Moskovit (p. 197) criticizes the adaptation for neglecting "unity of theme and logical continuity," objecting that the opening section (vv. 1–26), "with its prevailing topic of avarice combined with female sexual promiscuity, has little to do with the remainder of the poem, which deals with foolish or harmful extremes in satisfying male sexual passion." Pope, he thinks, starts off with "an obviously creative technique of imitation," from which he declines into "a nearly translational one." It is already apparent that I disagree with such a view. The feminizing of Horace's opening is not only consistent in the ways I have already remarked, but also (and partly for these reasons) with the poem itself, as a whole. Here is a foretaste of the "big game" (*matronam*) which Horace and Pope rebuke us for so foolishly and rashly aspiring to when we would be safer and therefore saner to content ourselves with "Frigates of the second Rate." Women—high or low—are, after all, what it is all about. And avarice, as much as lust, is a part of their culpability in the crime. Pope displays, in reality, a high level of sophistication and sense of design in his adaptation; and, as I hope to show, a great deal of wit in rendering his poem something more than a mere translation.

20. Moskovit has remarked a number of Pope's adaptations. See pp. 195–196, 198. To his citations of Pope's particularizations of Horace may be added these: *hoc genus omne*—"all the Court . . . and half the Town" (3); *hic, ille, hunc* (41–44)—"Monsieur" and "good Sir *George*" (53, 55); *quid*

The imitation loses no time asserting its own authority. Wit and lampoon converge at once in the transformation of Horace's *Quippe Benignus erat* (said of Tigellius) to the boldly ambiguous declaration of what it is for Nan Oldfield to be *benigna:*

> Engaging *Oldfield!* who, with Grace and Ease,
> Could joyn the Arts, to ruin, and to please.   [5–6]

Such heightening, variously enforced, lights up the whole imitation. One sees it in the verses on Con Phillips:

> "Treat on, treat on," is her eternal Note,
> And Lands and Tenements go down her Throat   [13–14]

a vignette vastly more vivid than Horace's *ingrata . . . ingluvie* or *'Sordidus, atque animi quod parvi nolit haberi,'/Respondet.*[21] One sees it likewise in the metaphorical re-creation of Horace's straightforward and literal *sunt qui nolint tetigisse,* etc. [28–30]:

> Some feel no Flames but at the *Court* or *Ball,*
> And others hunt white Aprons in the *Mall.*   [37–38]

It multiplies Horace's *mimae* (v. 56, the actress to whom Marsaeus gives his patrimony) into a veritable bed of actresses:

> To *Palmer's* Bed no Actress comes amiss,
> He courts the whole *Personae Dramatis*   [71–72]

Intensification is especially effective in the adaptation of Horace's *Adde huc . . . turpia celet* [83–85]:

> And *secondly,* how innocent a *Belle*
> Is she who shows what Ware she has to sell;
> Not Lady-like, displays a milk-white Breast,
> And hides in sacred Sluttishness the rest.   [108–111]

---

vis tibi, etc. (69)—"Sir *Robert!* or Sir *Paul!"* (88); *Altera*—Mother Needham's (133); *Cantat*—"as *Sucklyn* sings" (139). Substitutions are many, as already noted, including, in addition, Bathurst (158) for *Philodemus* and Liddel, Jefferys, and Onslow (178) for *Fabio.*

21. Does Pope, in addition, play upon the first word of Horace's *cur atque parentis* for Con's opening exclamation, "A sneaking Dog I hate"?

Pope adds to Horace's undenominated prostitute the playful
irony of "Belle," against which he plays off (again to Horace's
undenominated matron) the sarcastic paradox, "Lady-like,"
building up to the devastating oxymoron, "sacred Sluttishness."

Where, as we see, Horace is generally content with the literal,
Pope turns reflexively to metaphor, as in the handy pairing of
figurative with literal in the following:

> . . . O crus, o brachia! verum
> Depugis, nasuta, brevi latere, ac pede longo est.   [92–93]
>
> Goose-rump'd, Hawk-nos'd, Swan-footed, is my Dear?
> They'l praise her *Elbow, Heel,* or *Tip o'th Ear.*
>   [122–23]

Horace's *Matronae, praeter faciem, nil cernere possis* is made
more pointed: "A Lady's Face is all you see undress'd" (124).
Interdicta becomes "Charms more latent" (126) and *Custodes,
Lectica,* etc., "Spies, Guardians, Guests, old Women, Aunts, and
Cozens!"[22]

The uproar scene with which the poem ends finds Pope
intensifying his source with a burlesque of the kind of thing one
encounters in his own *Elegy* and *Eloisa* and in Restoration
She-Tragedy and picaresque story:

> From gleaming Swords no shrieking Women run;
> No wretched Wife cries out, *Undone! Undone!*
> Seiz'd in the Fact, and in her Cuckold's Pow'r,
> She kneels, she weeps, and worse! resigns her Dow'r.
> Me, naked me, to Posts, to Pumps they draw,
> To Shame eternal, or eternal Law.   [169–174]

---

22. V. 129. Cf. the annotation recorded in Butt, p. 85: "a famous
Stay-maker of this name [Cozens] . . . stiffens the *double-entendre* here
meant. . . ." It should not go unremarked either that in this line Pope gives
us an Alexandrine to go with the "obstacles by dozens" of the preceding
line.

There is even a touch of Restoration comedy in the hubbub, an echo of the surprises, or near surprises, in the cuckolding crises of that drama.

We have seen a hint of Swift in the macaronic rhyme quoted above (amiss-*Dramatis*), and we have remarked the Swiftian flavor of Pope's Moll and Jack, Peg and Jenny. Something too of Swift may account for the element of the boisterous in Pope's adaptation, the frankness and occasional impertinence of the style, and the impish delight with which it pursues its serious purpose. One of the episodes is particularly reminiscent of Swift, the anecdote of Cato's encounter with the rake emerging from the stews, soberly described in Horace, but here given a Swiftian burlesque turn—to which Pope adds what is almost certainly an implied joke on himself and the Dean:

> My Lord of L—n, chancing to remark
> A *noted Dean* much busy'd in the Park,
> "Proceed (he cry'd) proceed, my Reverend Brother,
> " 'Tis *Fornicatio simplex,* and no other:
> "Better than lust for Boys, with *Pope* and *Turk,*
> "Or others Spouses, like my Lord of [York][23]

Swift too, of course, liked a joke on himself, and that may also reflect his impingement on the adaptation.

Of the Restoration comic vein there is abundant evidence. We have caught a glimpse of it in the "Mall" (38) and in the cuckoldry that weaves in and out of the poem and that forms its climax. We see it too in the rendering of Horace's literal *moechos* (fornicators, adulterers) as "Cuckold-maker[s]" (48) and in the location of these offenders squarely in the "City." This impression is not lessened by the addition of venereal "Pangs" (51) to Horace's *dolore,* or by the substitution of a *Monsieur* and a "Sir *George*" (53, 55) for Horace's noncommittal *hics,*

---

23. Vv. 39–44. Cf. Swift's "An Excellent New Ballad" on the same subject (*Poems,* ed. Williams, II, 516 ff.).

illes, and *huncs.* The vein persists in the witty adaptation of Horace's *merx . . . in classe secunda: "trades* in *Frigates* of the second Rate."[24] And this particular vignette concludes with the alteration of *Matronam* to "Dame[s] of Quality," another reminder of the comedy of wit. It is possible, finally, that Pope's adaptation of Horace's example of horse-trading harks to that Prince of Restoration rakes, Charles. Pope makes an interesting change in Horace's *Regibus* (86) which points in that direction. In Horace the word signifies *great men,* in the sense of *wealthy.* Pope takes it back to its root meaning, *king,* playing, we may suppose, with the idea of certain English kings, like Charles especially, who traded as shrewdly in the female as in the equine form:

> Our ancient Kings (and sure those Kings were wise,
> Who judg'd themselves, and saw with their own Eyes)
> [112–113]

That those kings are then described as trading in war-horses is no hindrance, for the introductory couplet is nicely open-ended, and Pope has only recently (v. 82) alluded to Charles by name. Given that circumstance, and the subject of the poem, Charles could hardly ever be far out of mind.[25]

Of all the resources for adaptation in *Sober Advice,* the most notorious, however, if not the most conspicuous, is the *double-entendre,* itself reminiscent of the comedy of the last age. We have encountered it already, if we may trust the annotator, in

24. V. 62, italics mine. Maritime imagery for the sex and for sexual activity is common in Restoration comedy. Cf. Ariana and Gatty, of Courtall and Freeman, in Etherege's *She wou'd if she cou'd,* II, i, 73 ff. Also the sailing metaphor in Vanbrugh's *Relapse,* III, ii, and Mirabell's classic description of the entry of Millamant in *The Way of the World,* II, v. For the word *frigate* as applied to a woman, see Eric Partridge, *Dictionary of Slang and Unconventional English.*

25. For Charles's habit of judging with his own eyes, see the *Mémoires de la Vie du Comte de Gramont.* For further instances of the Restoration accent in *Sober Advice,* see *n.* 12 above.

the word *Cozens* of verse 129, where it is innocent enough; and earlier, where it is less innocent, in the "Flames" of verse 37 and the phrase "comes amiss" of verse 71. What is, unfortunately, too often overlooked about this much criticized device is that its use, like that of the metaphor, is as often a measure of "decency" as it is of witticism, enabling the poet, as Bolingbroke put it, to "weaken the images [rather] than to hurt chaste ears overmuch," though it is true enough that the device makes it possible to have it both ways, naughty as well as nice, witty as well as sober. But that, as we have said, is what the satiric genius requires, if it is to function at its most effective. Pope, at any rate, accomplishes some rather remarkable results with the device, which it would be difficult to show he ever really uses irresponsibly.

One of the brightest of his *doubles-entendres* is the first, in vv. 35–36:

> But diff'rent Taste in diff'rent Men prevails,
> And one is fired by Heads, and one by Tails.

Though it has no counterpart in Horace, this would, I think, be counted wit by him, mounting, as it does, the *jeu d'esprit* on a composition of gambling, lust, and the price of whoring, all expressed in a lively conceit.

Pope also triumphs in the alliance of metaphor and *double-entendre* with which he meets the challenge of Horace's *cunni albi* (36):

> . . . Nolim laudarier, inquit,
> Sic me, mirator, CUNNI CUPIENNIUS ALBI.

"'I should not care to be so praised, No, Sir,' says Cupiennius, admirer of *Cunni Albi*." Thus literally. Pope makes a conquest of it:

> May no such Praise (cries J——s) e'er be mine!
> J[efferie]s, who bows at *Hi[ll]sb[oro]w's hoary Shrine.*
> [45–46]

The *double-entendre* arises from a pun, of course, but the result is impressive under either rubric, for it illustrates how, at his best, Pope can fuse the scandalous and the serious without loss to either, and with enormous advantage to satiric penetration.

Toward the end of the poem Pope executes another skillful *double-entendre*. LEPOREM, says Horace,

> . . . venator ut alta
> In nive sectetur, positum sic tangere nolit   [105–106]

Or, as Pope put it,

> "The Hare once seiz'd the Hunter heeds no more
> The little Scut he so pursu'd before   [137–38]

Horace *leporem*, left at "hare" in Pope's first line, is wittily converted to the aptness of "scut" in the second.[26]

Verses 150–54 constitute a cluster of double meanings. The Bentleyan footnote to Horace's *Pavonem* (peacock) suggests that Pope was willing to have his *Pea-Chicks* so understood (*"meaning a* young *or* soft Piece, *Anglice* a Tid-bit").[27] Horace would, I think, have been pleased with Pope's "tight, neat Girl" for his own *Ancilla . . . verna* (maidservant), and candor will surely credit Pope for the distillation of *tument tibi cum inguina* through a tissue of ethical remonstrance, Pauline proverbialism, and *double-entendre*:

> Or, when a tight, neat Girl, will serve the Turn,
> In errant Pride continue stiff, and burn?[28]

The passage concludes with *double-entendre* contrived of good English homespun, rendering *parabilem amo venerem, facilemque* (119), "The Thing at hand is of all Things the *best*."[29]

26. See *scut* in Eric Partridge, *Shakespeare's Bawdy*.
27. Butt, p. 86*n*.
28. Vv. 151–152. Horace's own *tentigine* (118) seems susceptible of double meaning.
29. Other, less witty and in some cases less certain, *doubles-entendres* occur in vv. 9 ("Pay'd it down"), 74 ("draw him in"), 81 ("push'd . . . on"), 86

Part of the disaffection with Pope's *double-entendre* belongs, properly, not to the poem, but to the *Notae Bentleianae,* which have contributed much to the poem's disrepute. But this objection is not only misplaced, but blown out of all proportion to the evidence. The notes number only seven, of which two are entirely innocent (the first two), two others essentially neutral (those on *consule. Cunnum* and *testis caudamque salacem*), and a fifth—that on *Pavonem*—not only inoffensive, but actually amusing. Only two of the notes are strictly indecent, that on *cunni albi* and that on *dum futuo.* But however the notes are scored, it is a mistake to regard them as convicting Pope, for they are parodic and clearly designed to convict Bentley. Even where they exceed the known evidence, as in the pruriency of the admittedly smutty ones, they should probably be thought of as falling under the license of satire to discredit by implied or express attribution of reprehensible motive or traits, whether such are actually in evidence or not. This is Swift's way, we know, with dissenters and zealots, and it has been the way with satirists from Aristophanes on. In resorting to it Pope was simply availing himself of an ancient and much exercised license.

But the poem is, after all, a thing essentially apart from the notes, and there, by means of witty and tactful *double-entendre* and metaphor, apt allusion to Restoration comic symbolism, recourse to Swiftian facetiousness, and his own talent for happy descant and invention on Horace, Pope has appropriated *Satire* I. ii to his role of satiric moralist with a success that has too long gone unacknowledged.

In thus re-evaluating *Sober Advice* it is not a matter of pretending that the performance is not "racy." That it is, and that is precisely much of its virtue as satire. But the view of the poem as nasty or pornographic, as a libel or a private diversion, or even as

---

("shut out . . . let in"), 147–148 (*re* the "flowing Bowl"?), 150 ("Bedford-head"=bed's head?), 175 ("deep Tranquility"), and 177 ("the Dev'll in Hell").

an indifferent piece, is neither warrented nor just, and deserves discrediting. *Sober Advice* is, as I hope I have shown, a serio-comic poem, relevant to both the moral and satirical vision of its creator, and no mean specimen of his genius. It deserves to be restored to the study of Pope.

4

Plain Truth, dear MURRAY

W HEN, in 1738, Pope addressed his imitation of Horace's
Epistle I. vi to William Murray, he did not choose the
most obvious candidate for his favors of this sort. Murray was yet
to hold any of the offices that would later bring him into promi-
nence, though the prospects were evident enough. He had
argued impressively before Lords in 1733 and again in 1734 and
1737. In 1738, after Pope's poem, he won commendation for his
eloquence before the Commons in support of the merchant's
petition concerning Spanish maritime offenses. But these cre-
dentials in themselves would hardly qualify him for priority in
the list of those eligible for Pope's epistolary salutation.[1] Why
then was he so honored? Traditionally the explanation has been
assumed to be personal, as no doubt it is in part. But there is
reason to believe that something more than generosity was involved and that Pope's motive was as much political as anything
else.[2] Before consulting the evidence of this, it will be useful to
review the history, scant enough, of the relationship of Pope and
Murray up to the time of the poem.

1. Among the more obvious candidates for Pope's epistolary patronage was,
of course, Swift, who had been literally begging Pope for such notice. See his
letter of 3 September 1735, in *Corr.*, III, 492. Cf. too the letter dated
1732–33, in III, 343–344.

2. Of the genesis of the poem we know next to nothing, only that it was
published 23 January 1738, its copyright having been registered just over a
week before. See Griffith, No. 476. From the correspondence comes only the
ghost of a hint. In September of 1737 James Watson published, or threatened

If we can believe Lord Campbell, Pope first met Murray while the latter was still a student at Westminster School, sometime between 1718 and 1723.

Pope . . . intuitively discovered the genius of this juvenile worshipper [as a child Murray had gotten the *Pastorals* by heart], was struck by his extraordinary accomplishments, agreeable manners, ingenuous countenance, and (it is said), above all, by the *silvery tones of his voice*. . . .[3]

Campbell tells us that Murray was introduced to Pope by his countryman Lord Marchmont, but it may be that the connection was also forwarded by Bishop Atterbury, who was still Dean of Westminster at the time and Pope's friend since at least 1713. Murray's family was Jacobite, and Campbell suspected of the Westminster enrollment that "Atterbury had said a good word for the scion of a noble Jacobite family. . . ."[4] Whatever Atterbury's part, the introduction of Pope and Murray did not apparently bear the fruit of active friendship until at least some ten or twelve years later, when Murray took up residence at Lincoln's Inn (1730–32) and when Pope, according to tradition, undertook to tutor him in oratory.[5] It is just possible that Murray was

to publish, a pirated edition of Pope's letters (cf. Griffith, No. 470 and the note, II, 370). In mid-November Pope wrote to Nathaniel Cole, solicitor to the Stationers' Company, informing him that Mr. Murray had advised him to "file a bill" against Watson (*Corr.,* IV, 87). This suggestion of closeting with and indebtedness to Murray is the only thing resembling a clue to the poem's inception that we have, and it is obviously not enough.

3. John Lord Campbell, *The Lives of the Chief Justices of England* (London, 1849), II, 330. See also pp. 315–318. Murray's latest biographer, C. H. S. Fifoot, accepts this date of meeting. See *Lord Mansfield* (Oxford: Clarendon, 1936), p. 31.

4. Campbell, II, 316. See also Fifoot, p. 27. Pope would have found Murray's Jacobitical connection both attractive and disconcerting.

5. See Campbell, II, 330. Edward Foss, *A Biographical Dictionary of the Judges of England* (London, 1870), p. 469, implies, on what authority it is not clear, an intimacy between Murray and Pope from the outset. W. N. Welsby, on the other hand, says nothing of acquaintance, much less of

the "successful Youth" of the verses sent by Pope to Aaron Hill in September of 1731 and later reworded for the *Epistle to Arbuthnot*.[6] It is rather more possible that he was the attorney of that name mentioned by Pope in a letter to Lord Oxford in October of the same year.[7] Pope may, indeed, by this time not only have recognized and responded to Murray's talents but availed himself of them by way of legal counsel, as he did more than once later.[8] Campbell, at any rate, refers to visits exchanged between Twickenham and Lincoln's Inn as well as visits by Pope to Murray's new lodgings in No. 5 King's Bench Walk.[9] It was about 1736, apparently, that Murray met with the "disappointment in an affair of the heart" that, according to Campbell, led Pope to try "to cheer him" by addressing him in the imitation of Horace's *Ode to Venus* and *Nil admirari*.[10]

This record, obviously imperfect, is not improved by the want of correspondence between Murray and Pope, a fact that would be difficult to account for were it not that they lived close enough to one another to visit and so make correspondence unnecessary. That they did visit frequently is amply attested by Pope's letters to others. But this testimony does not reach further back than 1736, a fact strange enough, on the face of it, if they were, as Campbell declares, intimate before that date.[11]

---

friendship, prior to the 1730s. See *Lives of Eminent English Judges* (Philadelphia, 1846), p. 381 ff.

6. See *Corr.*, III, 226 and *n.* Sherburn is apparently mistaken in saying that at this time (1731) Murray had not yet been called to the bar. Bowles was apparently the first to associate the "successful Youth" with Murray. See *Works*, ed. Bowles, I, xc and VIII, 390.

7. *Corr.*, III, 236.

8. Beginning in November of 1737, in the matter of Watson's piracy. See *Corr.*, IV, 87–88, 203, 214, 245, 385 ff., 410 f., 425, 427.

9. Campbell, II, 330, 334. But see below, *n.* 11.

10. *Ibid.*, pp. 339–340.

11. The earliest allusion to visitation occurs 26 August 1736 (*Corr.*, IV, 29). For the record of subsequent visits (Pope to Murray) see *Corr.*, IV, 150, 175, 332, 380, 381, 383, 489, 498, 505; (Murray to Pope), 389, 431, 442.

After the evidence is sifted one is left with the conclusion that, however early the acquaintance of these two men and their respect for one another, the maturation of their friendship did not antedate the mid-thirties, and the explanation may, as we shall see, have as much to do with timing as with time.[12]

Of the imitation, Reuben Brower remarks the tonal variation on Horace, a magniloquence reminiscent of Hamlet and a heroic strain reminiscent of Dryden's Persius.[13] J. W. Tupper remarks the philosophical variation. Horace's was, he says,

a doctrine essentially pagan and not one that Pope could treat *con amore*. . . . It was hardly possible for the author of the *Essay on Man*, who professed to be a Christian apologist and thought his essay was a remarkable vindication of the ways of God to man, even to affect to make his own this piece of pagan philosophy. Further, Pope was not a man who could assume effectively even the appearance of indifference in either the greater or lesser concerns of life. . . . To remain consistent, therefore, with his preaching, he gives a serious tone to Horace's flippancy. . . . Pope's text . . . is not 'nil admirari,' as he announces . . . but the opposite.[14]

Tupper links the imitation to the ethical program of the thirties, and not improperly. But there is yet another, though not unrelated, source of the difference between the imitation and its model, and that is the pronounced political orientation of Pope's

12. In his first unmistakable reference to Murray (letter to Fortescue 26 August 1736) Pope says, "He is one of the few people whom no man that knows, can forget, or not esteem." (*Corr.*, IV, 29) I have not been able to discover the authority for A. W. Ward's statement (*The Poetical Works of Alexander Pope*, Gladstone ed., 1896, p. 306*n*) that "Murray had originally won the gratitude of [Pope] by his defence of the *Essay on Man* from the attacks of Crousaz." The attribution reads rather like a mistake for Warburton.

13. Brower, *Alexander Pope*, pp. 309–310.

14. Tupper, p. 212.

version.[15] Pope is now in the thick of his campaign against corruption in Court and Ministry (a preoccupation to which this particular Horatian epistle lends itself perfectly), and I would suggest that it is this fact as much as anything else which led him to address the imitation to Murray—the hope to engage his promising young protege not only on the side of virtue (including disdain for the misfortunes of love) but on the side of patriotism as well. Pope, in short, would create another Boy Patriot.[16]

Party rivalry for political and literary talent was as keen in the thirties as ever, and Murray must have seemed to Whig, Tory, and Patriot alike a highly desirable catch. Campbell reports in fact that between 1730 and 1732, the first years of Murray's career at the bar,

His friends were most afraid, from his literary connections and propensities, that he would be induced to relax his resolution to raise himself by the law, and that he would attempt authorship or prematurely mix in political strife.[17]

15. An orientation as yet unremarked, so far as I know. Brower seems vaguely aware of it, and yet not. He links the poem with the political motive of the *Augustus* and declares its view of England "darker" than that of the earlier poem, but then declares that "the judgment implied [in it] is characteristically moral rather than political." See p. 309. Horace's poem is by no stretch of the imagination political. Its only reference of that sort (vv. 49–55)—which may incidentally have first drawn Pope's eye to the usefulness of the epistle for imitation at this juncture—is simply one of the several alternatives of behavior canvassed as available to Horace's man of detachment.

16. That Pope saw Murray in terms of the Boy Patriots is suggested by a letter to Swift 17 May 1739, in which he links Murray with Polwarth and Cornbury: "There is a Lord Cornbury, a Lord Polwarth, a Mr Murray, & one or two more [Lyttelton and West?], with whom I would never fear to hold out against all the corruption of the world." *Corr.,* IV, 178.

17. Campbell, II, 333. Murray at this time, according to Campbell, "actually declined an offer made to bring him immediately into parliament. . . ." On the lure of literature, see also Welsby, pp. 383–384.

About the time of Pope's imitation of *Epistle* I. vi, "Both parties
in the state were eager to enlist him in their ranks." At this
point, as Campbell says,

there were very few professed Tories, and still fewer avowed Jacob-
ites. Politicians struggling for power, almost all coming within the
general denomination of Whigs, were divided into the adherents and
the enemies of Sir Robert Walpole. Murray warily refused to
join either the one class or the other.[18]

He preferred, in Campbell's words, "to be guided by the sentiment of Pope, that 'the man who may have the good-will of all
parties is guilty of folly if he becomes a partisan.' "[19] If Campbell
has put words in Pope's mouth, he has not substantially misrep-
resented him, for Pope was always opposed to partisanship pure
and simple. But by this time he was in open sympathy and
counsel with the Opposition and was doing his best to advance
the nonpartisan ideal of the Patriots. Given even a fraction of
the intimacy with Murray claimed by Campbell and others,
Pope must have been acutely sensible of the desirability of
attaching his talent and potential to the Patriot Opposition, or at
least of preserving him, as Fifoot said of Atterbury's role, "from
Whig contamination. . . ."[20] And though Murray would in a
few years enter the government under Whig sponsorship, he
was at this time still uncommitted and would in fact, only a little
after Pope's epistle, appear in Commons in opposition to Walpole in the affair of Jenkins's Ear. Pope had, in short, not only
motive but opportunity and special advantage for cultivating
Murray's political sympathies in 1737 and 1738. Let us see how
the poem itself supports the likelihood that he did.[21]

18. Campbell, II, 345.
19. *Ibid.*, p. 346.
20. Fifoot, p. 27.
21. The truth is, of course, that Murray never really yielded to party. He
was, as Fifoot observes (pp. 37–38), "never quite happy in political life.
Prudent to the point of timidity, he was too cool or too calculating to accept

In searching for the real motive of Pope's address we must bear in mind that a recommendation to virtue would have seemed to any but the modest Murray himself a gratuity of the worst sort on the part of the epistolist, since all accounts of Murray stress his moral rectitude from his earliest years. For Pope to speak to him on such a subject therefore must be understood, at least on its face, as a form of compliment and not of counsel. It is equally apparent, however, that Pope's motive exceeds mere compliment. What we perceive instead, upon a close reading of the epistle, is a carefully couched appeal to Murray's well-known virtue to extend itself to considerations public as well as private, to enlist itself on the side of political morality; to resist the blandishments of Court and Ministry and to cast its lot with the patriotic Opposition. Pope will lose little time in broaching this his real subject of address to Murray.

After a brief opening in which he alludes to Murray's interest in oratory and his part in its cultivation, Pope subtly bends Horace in the direction he would guide Murray's thinking. Under his hand Horace's relatively casual question regarding the wonder due the heavens and that due the earth not only gains in philosophic and religious import but takes on political overtones indicative of his thematic drift and crucial to his rhetorical objective:

> This Vault of Air, this congregated Ball,
> Self-centered Sun, and Stars that rise and fall,
> There are, my Friend! whose philosophic eyes
> Look thro', and trust the Ruler with his Skies,
> To him commit the hour, the day, the year,
> And view this dreadful All without a fear.   [5–10]

---

without reserve the terms of any party, and his preference for a 'broad-bottomed administration' aroused the suspicion of less balanced and more ardent temperaments." It would have aroused applause, however, in the patriotic camp, and Murray's "broad-bottom" disposition suggests that the Bolingbroke-Pope-Patriot line made its impression on him after all.

Quite apart from their manifest invitation to piety and their reminder of the merits and differences of the great and the small, these lines adumbrate the specifically political aspect of the argument to follow, imaging as it were a heavenly (or celestial) court in which—unlike that earthly one of Hampton, where stars are political reward and where they rise and fall by political whim—the rising and falling of stars is according to orderly and beneficent principles and whose Ruler therefore, unlike a George, may be trusted and never feared. Pope will continue, as we shall see, to disclose his polemical intent in this oblique and gradual fashion.

Where Horace merely asks the question, "Quid censes munera Terrae?" etc., Pope, though he makes the contrast explicit, broaches his ultimate meaning synechdochically:

> Admire we then what Earth's low entrails hold ⎫
> Arabian shores, or Indian seas infold,   ⎬
> All the mad trade of Fools and Slaves for Gold? ⎭

The last line makes explicit, in terms of Pope's greater sensitivity, what is left at barest hint in Horace, the theme of venality, for Pope the prime symbol of ministerial and courtly default of ethical standard. In similar manner, with a significant backward glance at the stars of heaven, Pope spells out the Horatian *ludicra,* or shows, which, along with "plausus, & amici dona Quiritis," become

> . . . Popularity, or Stars and Strings?
> The Mob's applauses, or the gifts of Kings?   [14–15]

Though this calls a string a String and invokes the derogative of *Kings,* it still might pass for the innocence of a cancellation of extremes were it not for the couplet that follows, where, for Horace's "Quo spectanda modo?" Pope brings the issue squarely round to politics at last:

> Say with what eyes we ought at Courts to gaze,
> And pay the Great our homage of Amaze?   [16–17]

This of course is a question directed as much to Murray personally as to the common reader. Murray was, after all, as Campbell
reminds us, treading on "the brink of all we hate," and Pope
would rescue him, for both their sakes.

Though he has now fairly tipped his hand, Pope continues to
address his argument with the same tactical subtlety with which
he broached it. Having, for example, next followed Horace
closely enough to the effect that "Whether we dread, or whether
we desire,/In either case, believe me, we admire," Pope bids his
private and public reader alike:

> Go then, and if you can, admire the state
> Of beaming diamonds, and reflected plate.   [28–29]

The strategy is typically ingenuous. The first line enjambs, and
its rhyme word is a noun signifying *condition,* but the line lends
itself easily to the impression of end-stop on a word signifying
the body politic. That, at any rate, Pope is still thinking of Court
and politics and Murray is evident from what follows:

> Be struck with bright Brocade, or Tyrian Dye,
> Our Birth-day Nobles splendid Livery:
> If not so pleas'd, at Council-board rejoyce,
> To see their Judgments hang upon thy Voice;
> From morn to night, at Senate, Rolls, and Hall,
> Plead much, read more, dine late, or not at all.   [32–37]

In the original of this, Horace speaks, not of politics, but of
wealth, pride and business. Only his reference to the pleasure of
being beheld while one holds forth in speech ("Gaude, quod
spectant oculi te mille loquentem") furnishes Pope the basis for
this additional allusion to Murray's interest in oratory and to his
success in it before the House of Lords. Ostensibly designed to

compliment Murray, the allusion is calculated at the same time
to warn him of the cost in vanity of following his talent where it
could so easily lead him.

When Pope next alludes to Murray's unhappy love affair, that
too is marshaled in terms subtly political in import:

> But wherefore all this labour, all this strife?
> For Fame, for Riches, for a noble Wife?
> Shall One whom Nature, Learning, Birth, conspir'd
> To form, not to admire, but be admir'd,
> Sigh, while his Chloë, blind to Wit and Worth,
> Weds the rich Dulness of some Son of earth?[22]

Nature, learning, birth, wit and worth, form a cluster of virtues
Pope and the Opposition were fond of invoking against the
ambition (Fame), riches, social climbing (noble Wife), and
dullness of the Whig establishment.

In what follows Pope accomplishes an eloquent, pointed, and
highly significant adaptation of Horace on the futility of one of
those Whiggish vanities, fame:

> Yet Time ennobles, or degrades each Line;
> It brighten'd CRAGS's, and may darken thine:
> And what is Fame? the Meanest have their day,
> The Greatest can but blaze, and pass away.
> Grac'd as thou art, with all the Pow'r of Words,
> So known, so honour'd, at the House of Lords;
> Conspicuous Scene! another yet is nigh,
> (More silent far) where Kings and Poets lye;
> Where MURRAY (long enough his Country's pride)
> Shall be no more than TULLY, or than HYDE!   [44–53]

To appreciate what, beyond the obvious, Pope is here saying to
Murray, we must recall, as Pope doubtless expected Murray to
do, what the poet had said before to Craggs.[23]

---

22. Vv. 38–43. But for the attribution of dullness it is tempting to see in
"Son of earth" a covert allusion to the Norfolk squire, Sir Robert.

23. James Craggs the younger, d. 1721, one of Pope's early Whig friends,
Secretary at War in 1717, Secretary of State in 1718. His early death, from

STATESMAN, yet Friend to Truth! of Soul sincere,
In Action faithful, and in Honour clear!
Who broke no promise, serv'd no private end,
Who gain'd no Title, and who lost no Friend,
Ennobled by Himself, by All approv'd,
Prais'd, wept, and honour'd, by the Muse he lov'd.

Composed sometime after Addison's death in June 1719, these
verses originally appeared, in slightly different form, at the conclusion of *To Mr. Addison, Occasioned by his Dialogue on
Medals* (1720). In the form quoted above they appear in Pope's
epitaph for Craggs's monument in Westminster Abbey, first
printed in 1727.[24] But Pope had also written an *Epistle to James
Craggs*, perhaps as early as 1718, though not published until
1735, a date more immediate to the *Epistle to Murray* and thus
to its addressee's recall. It contains lines even more to the point
of Pope's present purpose:

All this thou wert; and being this before,
Know, Kings and Fortune cannot make thee more.
Then scorn to gain a Friend by servile ways,
Nor wish to lose a Foe these Virtues raise;
But candid, free, sincere, as you began,
Proceed --- a Minister, but still a Man;
Be not (exalted to whate'er degree)
Asham'd of any Friend, not ev'n of Me.
The Patriot's plain, but untrod path pursue;
If not, 'tis I must be asham'd of You.[25]

---

smallpox, grieved Pope. "There never lived," he wrote Caryll, "a more worthy
nature, a more disinterested mind, a more open and friendly temper. . . ."
(*Corr.*, II, 73; see also pp. 134, 243.)

24. See Norman Ault and John Butt, editors, *Minor Poems* (Twickenham ed.), pp. 202–206, 281–282. Also p. 465, for a variant alluding to royal
gratitude that was removed by Pope before the Addisonian version first
appeared in Addison's *Works*, 1721.

25. Ault and Butt, *Minor Poems*, pp. 209–210. See also *A Dialogue*, p.
211. Murray must have seemed to Pope a kind of second Craggs, like the

Nor are the references to Tully and Hyde in the passage from
Murray merely adventitious. Tully is intended most immediately
of course to call up the idea of the orator, but he is also calculated to evoke a cluster of values and virtues ethical, social and
political.[26] Hyde, apart from his relevance to the Jacobitical
allegiance of Murray's family, was himself a patriot after another
fashion. Like Cicero too, he was the subject of senatorial exile,
the beholder of civil strife, and the victim finally, though not
fatally, of political ingratitude and jealousy. Like that of Craggs,
these names are calculated to flatter and to warn at once, not
simply as *memento mori* but as call to duty. Pope knew what
was in a name, and it is characteristic of him to distill, in this
fashion, whole arguments in its narrow room. To be no more
than Tully or than Hyde is, in short, not simply to be dead, but
to be the victim of political treachery.[27]

But there are patriots in hand as well as in memory, and after
a by-blow at Ward, the quack patronized by the King, Pope
invokes one of these:

---

latter young, honorable, talented, and obviously destined for political place
and responsibility.

26. The parallels between Murray and Tully are many, as Pope was
shrewdly aware. Both were successful lawyers, both distinguished politicians,
both orators who became wealthy, both scholars with a literary penchant, both
nonpartisan and marked by a certain timidity of character. Conyers Middleton
was to say of Cicero a few years later (1741), "As to his political conduct, no
man was ever a more determined patriot, or a warmer lover of his country.
. . . His general view . . . was always . . . to support the peace and liberty
of the Republic, in that form and constitution of it which their ancestors had
delivered down to them. . . . it was his constant aim to unite the different
orders of the state into one common interest, and to inspire them with a
mutual confidence in each other. . . ." (*Life of Marcus Tullius Cicero*
[London, 1810], III, 392–393.) This describes almost exactly the philosophy
and sentiment animating the Patriots under George II.

27. Warburton and Bowles both failed to recognize the subtlety of Pope's
invocation of names in this place. See their notes on vv. 52, 53. Other editors,
innocent of their sins of commission, are no better in respect to the sin of
omission.

> Would ye be blest? despise low Joys, low Gains;
> Disdain whatever CORNBURY disdains;
> Be Virtuous, and be happy for your pains.   [60–62]

The exhortation could scarcely be more pointed. Cornbury, great grandson of the HYDE invoked already, was one of the boy patriots, in whose posture of Opposition Pope was hoping to steer Murray.[28] In this brief passage, moreover, guilt-by-association, innocence-by-association, and virtue blend in an indivisible definition and appeal.

When, next, Pope follows Horace on the subject of *regina Pecunia* (v. 69 ff.), he gives political significance to that theme also,[29] making the connection explicit when, in vv. 83–84 he substitutes the Prince of Wales for Horace's Cappadocian king:

> Believe me, many a German Prince is worse,
> Who proud of Pedigree, is poor of Purse.[30]

But the political reorientation of Horace is served even more conveniently by the passage which follows, on *species et gratia,* which, though it means neither, Pope renders "Pow'r and Place." If, says Horace, show and recognition be your idea of a good life, why then buy a slave to prompt you on names, to nudge you when to extend the hand, and to advise you—as, for example, that such an one has influence in the Fabian, another in the Veline tribe, or this one will give the fasces where he will or snatch the curule ivory as he pleases. You need then but apply the epithet "Brother" or "Father," according to the age, amiably

28. For the account of Cornbury's declining to be bought by a pension, see Spence, I, 145.

29. That was easy enough of course. On venality as Opposition political capital, see Bolingbroke's *Remarks on the History of England,* Letter XIV; *Dissertation upon Parties,* including the Dedication; *A Letter on the Spirit of Patriotism,* and *The Idea of a Patriot King.*

30. Alluding to the quarrel over the Prince's allowance, a cause the Opposition made its own.

adopting each to your bosom.[31] What in Horace is at most a picture of affluent vanity and policy, Pope makes pointedly Courtly and Ministerial:

> But if to Pow'r and Place your Passion lye,
> If in the Pomp of Life consist the Joy;
> Then hire a Slave, (or if you will, a Lord)
> To do the Honours, and to give the Word;
> Tell at your Levee, as the Crouds approach,
> To whom to nod, whom take into your Coach,
> Whom honour with your hand: to make remarks,
> Who rules in Cornwall, or who rules in Berks;
> "This may be troublesome, is near the Chair;
> "That makes three Members, this can chuse a May'r."
> Instructed thus, you bow, embrace, protest,
> Adopt him Son, or Cozen at the least,
> Then turn about, and laugh at your own Jest.   [97–109]

There can be little question about the cast of characters here: a King, a Vice-Chamberlain, and a Prime Minister. It is George who, with the possible exception of the last three lines, lurks behind the mask of the nonce addressee. Hervey is as surely the Lord (and *slave:* Pope's terms are characteristically squinting) who advises at the Levee and Coach,[32] and it is he or Sir Robert or both who are the Machiavel of electoral know-how. The image is unpalatable enough in the Latin, where it is only remotely political in concept; here, where it is exclusively so, it is wholly unsavory, especially in the culminating verse, where Pope converts Horace's humorous *facetus* into the crudity of a politician's jest at his own hypocrisy.

With the character of the Glutton (Russel) Pope relaxes the political allusion, but brings it around again, less emphatically but no less surely, in his elaboration of Horace's allusion to

31. A free rendering of vv. 50–55, beginning Mercemur *servum* and concluding *ita quemque* facetus *adopta.*

32. For his own account of this role see Hervey, *passim.*

Ulysses' voluptuous Ithacans. The result is an indictment of debauchery clearly aimed at ministerial, courtly, and perhaps royal game:

> Or shall we ev'ry Decency confound,
> Thro' Taverns, Stews, and Bagnio's take our round,
> Go dine with Chartres, in each Vice out-do
> K—l's lewd Cargo, or Ty—y's Crew,
> From Latian Syrens, French Circaean Feasts,
> Return well travell'd, and transform'd to Beasts,
> Or for a Titled Punk, or Foreign Flame,
> Renounce our Country, and degrade our Name? [118–125]

This is partly commonplace to be sure—the Italianate gentleman of Renaissance complaint, the rake tourist of Pope's own *Dunciad*—and as such it serves the strictly ethical aspect of Pope's discourse. But it is also politically topical and allusive, proceeding on a kind of ladder principle, beginning at a lower rung and ascending all the way to the top. Chartres is the corrupt political minion, runner of Sir Robert and defender of the faithless.[33] Kinnoull, as Tory peer gone bad, serves not only to raise the indictment to the level of aristocracy but to afford Pope the rhetorical advantage of displaying his impartiality by revealing himself, Whig or Tory, To VIRTUE ONLY and HER FRIENDS, A FRIEND. Tyrawley was, like Kinnoull (ultimately), a Walpole appointee, whose licentiousness was not only condoned but, in his case, rewarded by promotion in the military.[34] Though he names no more names, it is almost certain that Pope mounts the final rung in his last couplet:

> Or for a Titled Punk, or Foreign Flame,
> Renounce our Country, and degrade our Name.

33. See the biographical note, Butt, p. 351.
34. Tyrawley, made aid-de-camp to George II in 1727, was promoted to brigadier-general in 1735. He was subsequently promoted grade by grade until, in 1763, he was made field marshal.

Walmoden, George's visits abroad, his contempt for, as well as embarrassment to, England—all these would shine through the wily cadence of this covert line.

The conclusion of the poem catches up the indictment in allusions of felicitous and telling contrast. The reference to Wimlot, for Horace's Mimnermus, recalls Pope's indulgent attitude toward the Stuart Court in the *Epistle to Augustus,* a court which, for all its faults, Pope always viewed nostalgically alongside that of Hanover. The reference to Swift, ancient foe of Whiggery and Walpole, restates the contrast in more nearly contemporary terms. To laugh and love—the composite, ideally viewed, of Restoration and Queen Anne virtues—are, after all, the true and innocent outlets of man's humanity, and are here, as in the *Augustus* (vv. 139–152), evoked in significant contrast to the crudity of Hanoverian conduct.

It is apparent that, as Tupper said, *Epistle* I. vi is, in Pope's hands, anything but a philosophy of detachment, that instead of *nil admirari* it proclaims just the opposite—the necessity of wonder in the present, Hanoverian, state of affairs. Under the pretence of following Horace, Pope has actually drawn the corruption of a present Court and Ministry and addressed the portrait to a young man, ripe for its ravening maw, in the hope, not alone of rescuing him, but of enlisting him in its Opposition.

5

In the Manner of Dr. Swift

IN 1738 and 1739, March and May respectively, Pope published "completions" of two pieces left only partially imitated by Swift: *The Sixth Satire of the Second Book* and *The Seventh Epistle of the First Book*.[1] Swift's part of the former is all the poem down to the fable of the city mouse and the country mouse, with its proem, which Pope added in his reprint of 1738.[2] Of the epistle Swift did the latter part, Pope supplying eighty-four lines corresponding to Horace's opening.

On the strength of references to August and an age "Near fifty," Professor Butt dates the composition of the epistle in the autumn of 1737.[3] Of this evidence the former, having Horatian precedent,[4] is scarcely admissable, while the latter, though admittedly less easy to challenge, is not so decisive as to preclude all

1. The satire appeared originally as "HORACE, Lib. 2 Sat. 6" in *Miscellanies. The Last Volume,* 1727. See Griffith, No. 479. Swift's part dates from the Letcombe period (1714). His "Part of the Seventh Epistle of the First Book of Horace Imitated" first appeared in 1713. For Pope's addition, see Griffith, No. 507.

2. Lines 9–28 of the "completed" poem have been taken by Courthope and Griffith as also Pope's, by Harold Williams as Swift's. Though I share John Butt's uncertainty (p. 248), I incline to the view of Williams. For Swift's part of both imitations, see *Poems,* ed. Williams, I, 197–198 and 169–170.

3. Butt, note, p. 269.

4. *Sextilem,* v. 2. Pope's "Dog-days" (v. 15) correspond also to Horace's *dum ficus prima calorque* (v. 5) and perhaps to his *febris* (v. 9).

debate. It is not, to begin with, unrelated to another conjecture about the epistle which might have some bearing on its reliability:

> When Pope imitated Horace's first epistle to Maecenas he addressed it to Bolingbroke, which argues that this imitation of another epistle to Maecenas may have been addressed to Bolingbroke as well. Lines 12 and 82 ["a thin Court that wants your Face," "Our old Friend Swift"] might be quoted in frail support of this view; on the other hand, Bolingbroke had few favours to bestow in the seventeen-thirties (1.21), and was not besieged by fools with compliments (1.29).[5]

There is, as Professor Butt confesses, a problem of attribution here, though not perhaps what he takes it to be. It is a question of how one reads the exceptions he points out, and that in turn is a question of how one reads the verses as a whole. There can, I think, be little doubt that Bolingbroke figures in this epistolary address, but there can be no less doubt that someone else figures too—however inconsistently with Horace and with history—and that is Harley. Pope is, after all, imitating Swift, and not alone in style but partly in person, assuming not only Swift's manner but occasionally his thought as well *and* his epistolary occasion, a word with Harley. No one can read *Ep*. I. vii (Pope's part) and escape the impression of a double perspective: that of Pope in the thirties on the one hand and that of Swift in the teens on the other. One feels the force of an allusion historical as well as stylistic, as if Pope were concerned not merely to experiment with Swift's idiom but to evoke his context as well, to allude to the days of Anne as well as those of Hanover, to view either in fact through the lens of the other and so focus the difference. The point of view in the epistle hovers between that of the early Swift and that of the later Pope, not simply juxtaposing the two, but superimposing now one, now the other, with the effect, as it

5. Butt, pp. 268–269n.

were, of mapping the discrepancies. We may observe briefly how this works before returning directly to the question of composition date.

The opening lines are at once in the spirit of Swift and Harley and inappropriate to the later Pope and Bolingbroke:

> 'Tis true, my Lord, I gave my word,
> I would be with you, June the third;
> Chang'd it to August, and (in short)
> Have kept it—as you do at Court.

These verses are perhaps as Swiftian in accent as any Pope ever wrote and their reference to Court is obviously applicable to Harley alone. Applied to Bolingbroke, not only would they make no sense on the score of Court, but none in respect to verses 2 and 3 as well, for Pope is hardly to be thought of as having committed himself to a visit abroad, and Bolingbroke, who in fact visited *him*, did not do so until mid 1738. By these same tokens, the "thin Court that wants your Face" will apply as well, if not better, to Harley after his dismissal as to Bolingbroke after his; and the "Bard" of v. 17 as easily to Swift as to Pope. On the other hand, if we take the "W* and H*" of v. 14 to refer to Ward and Henley, the perspective has obviously shifted to a view more favorable to Bolingbroke than to Harley. Professor Butt himself has pointed out the difficulties of associating vv. 21 and 29 with Bolingbroke, though of course they fit Swift and Harley perfectly well.

The double perspective, which as we have seen is not altogether wanting in the first forty-odd verses, becomes most noticeable in vv. 43–50:

> I hope it is your Resolution
> To give me back my Constitution!
> The sprightly Wit, the lively Eye,
> Th'engaging Smile, the Gaiety,
> That laugh'd down many a Summer's Sun,

And kept you up so oft till one;
And all that voluntary Vein,
As when Belinda rais'd my Strain.

The first couplet is an extraordinary specimen of Pope's mastery of ambiguity and paronomasy. It takes off from Horace's reference to his *youthful* constitution:

quod si me noles usquam discedere, reddes
forte latus, nigros angusta fronte capillos,
etc.[6]

This Pope both retains and, by a form of pun, alters. As a reference to youth, it fits Swift and Harley nicely, though of course it will also fit the later Pope and Bolingbroke. But as a reference to constitution in the political sense, it is obviously keyed to Pope, Bolingbroke, and the thirties. The difference, it is important to note, is not merely verbal or witty; it is significant, or thematic, as well. It spells, at least for Pope, the distinction between an age of innocence and an age of bitter experience, a time when *constitution* could mean nothing more sinister than good health and another when it had come to mean something as desperate as liberty. A similar thematic dimension will be seen to characterize all the instances of double perspective in the poem.

The next four lines, beginning with the "sprightly Wit" and ending with the "Summer's Sun," while they would not be incapable of application to Swift, especially the last two, are fairly obviously intended to represent Pope himself. We know, from other testimony, about Pope's eye,[7] and Spence tells us that in his early life Pope was "said by persons most intimate with him

6. Horace, vv. 25–26 ff.
7. Cf. Reynold's account as recorded in James Prior, *Life of Edmond Malone,* quoted in W. K. Wimsatt, *The Portraits of Alexander Pope* (New Haven: Yale University Press, 1965), p. xxv; also Johnson's account, *Lives of the Poets,* ed. G. B. Hill (Oxford, 1905), III, 197. Pope himself alludes to his *"Eye"* in the *Epistle to Arbuthnot,* v. 118.

to have been excessively gay and lively."[8] Belinda of course admits of no debate. But if the lines are Pope and Bolingbroke, they are Pope at least of the Scriblerus days and nights, when Harley was occasional guest at the festivals, and when Swift as well as Pope kept him up so oft till one. Those were the days of freedom, the *voluntary* days, now lost, unless Bolingbroke and the Patriots can recall them.

The anecdote of the Weasel (vv. 51–58) is again in the right Swiftian vein, though its "Application" (especially at the outset) is just as clearly in the Popeian. Likewise, "South-sea Subscriptions" (v. 65) are reminiscent of Harley, while "Liberty" and "Independency" (vv. 66, 70) bespeak Bolingbroke and the later Pope. "Near fifty, and without a wife," on which the dating of the poem is made to depend, while it fits Pope in obvious ways, would, it should be noted, fit a Harleian Swift too, who was forty-six in 1713.

Toward the end, preparatory to giving over in favor of Swift, Pope abandons the double perspective for simple fact. The "Paternal Cell,"

> A little House, with Trees a-row,
> And like its Master, very low,

is the Binfield of his own father and childhood. Then, to "set this matter full before you," he lets "Our old Friend Swift" present "his Story."

Bolingbroke is indeed then addressed in the epistle, but, as we have seen, not alone. To the extent, however, that his address is relevant to the dating of the poem, it would seem more appropriate to a later date than the autumn of 1737. Bolingbroke was Pope's house guest during the latter half of 1738 and more likely then than earlier to have excited a reprieve of epistolary address. Add to this, and to the other considerations proposed, the likeli-

8. Spence, I, 6.

hood that *Sat.* II. vi was itself composed in late 1737, and there would seem to be grounds for revising the conjectured date of *Ep.* I. vii. It will be useful to review briefly Pope's activities during the whole period.

In 1737 Pope was busy trying to pry his letters loose from an ailing, forgetful, and often morose Swift, writing often to him and to the Earl of Orrery about them. On 31 May Swift wrote to Pope on the subject and in the course of the letter reproached him for failing to memorialize their friendship by the address of a verse epistle.[9] On 23 July Orrery wrote to the Dean from London:

> Your commands are obeyed long ago. Dr. *King* has his cargo, Mrs. *Barber* her conversation, and Mr. *Pope* his letters. To-morrow [Sunday] I pass with him at *Twickenham:* the *olim meminisse* will be our feast. Leave *Dublin* and come to us.[10]

By April of 1738 Pope was writing to Allen about the first dialogue of the *Epilogue,* and in July Lyttelton apparently refers, in a letter to Pope, to its companion piece.[11] Bolingbroke was, as we have said, Pope's guest from the latter date until April 1739, during which time there must have been much talk of the Dean. The two of them apparently wrote Swift jointly on 25 July (the letter is lost), and in his reply (August) Swift disclaimed some compliments they had paid his verse and praised Pope's second dialogue. On 25 September, in a brief note to Orrery, Pope declared that he was returning a copy sent him of the *Verses on the Death of Dr. Swift,* on which he proceeded to make brief comment.[12] During October and November Pope was being solicited in behalf of the Opposition and the Prince of

9. *Corr.,* IV, 71–72.
10. *Ibid.,* pp. 81–82.
11. *Ibid.,* pp. 93, 109; see also *n.* 1, p. 109.
12. *Ibid.,* p. 130.

Wales. In a letter to Burlington, 19 December, he writes that his and Bolingbroke's "constant Toast is, *Libertati & Amicitiae*," indicating a not surprising perseverance of political fervor.[13]

In the absence of positive evidence, it is clearly possible to place Pope's imitations at almost any point along this calendar: at the remembrance of things past on the visit of Orrery in July of thirty-seven (especially since Swift had finally surrendered his letters); at the time of Pope's and Bolingbroke's compliment to the Dean on his poetry in July of thirty-eight; or during the Opposition courtship in October and November of the same year. Pope was throughout in a political mood, Swift was bidding for literary notice, and, after mid-1738, Bolingbroke was there to link the two and to break the Sabbath of Pope's days with incitements to rhyme.

Since, however, there is reason to believe that vv. 143–144 of *Sat.* II. vi allude to the rival Court of late 1737 and to place the composition of the satire in the wake of that scandal,[14] since it is not likely that Pope would undertake two Swiftian exercises at the same time, and since there is no particular reason to place the composition of the epistle earlier and no compulsive evidence for dating it in the fall of 1737, I am inclined to place it sometime after mid–1738, when Bolingbroke became Pope's guest at Twickenham.

The imitations have excited little attention, and that, rather unfortunately, has been directed chiefly to the Swiftian comparison. The verdict in that regard has not been favorable to Pope, and no doubt justly enough, though not necessarily for the reasons usually given. This question, as we shall see, is not unrelated to that of epistolary design discussed in connection with the dating of the poems.

13. *Ibid.*, p. 153.
14. See below, pp. 99–100 and notes 26, 27.

Warton early remarked that "the colloquial and burlesque style and measure of Swift, here adopted, did not suit the genius and manner of our Author, who frequently *falls back,* as was natural, from the familiar into his own more laboured, high, and pompous manner."[15] Even Swift disclaimed the resemblance, at least in one case, though Pope himself felt that he had approximated the Dean's style rather well. Under the date 1742 Spence records Pope to that effect:

When I had filled up this Epistle, begun by Swift, I sent it to the Doctor, and thought I had hit his style exactly, for it was familiar, lively, and with odd rhymes. The Doctor had a very different opinion of it, and did not think it at all a right imitation of his style.[16]

While there can be no serious quarrel with the verdict, either as reported by the Dean or by Warton, there is room to question the customary interpretation of this anecdote. It is generally supposed to refer to Pope's part of *Sat.* II. vi. Harold Williams so regards it, as does James M. Osborn.[17] But the evidence is far from conclusive, and there are reasons for believing that Pope's remarks refer instead to *Ep.* I. vii. A consideration of this matter is not, at any rate, irrelevant to the issue of Pope's success as an imitator of Swift.

Presumably the attribution to *Sat.* II. vi is based ultimately on the expressions "filled up" and "begun by Swift," on the assumption that by the former Pope meant *finished* (in the sense of

15. Quoted in Bowles, VI, sg. B2. Cf. A. W. Ward: "With Pope the attempt to write in Swift's style was a mere *tour de force,* which he could indeed carry out with success through a few lines, but not further, without relapsing into his own more elaborate manner. Swift's marvelous precision and *netteté* of expression are something very different from Pope's pointed and rhetorical elegance." (*The Poetical Works of Alexander Pope,* from the Globe edition, revised and enlarged [New York: Crowell, 1896], p. 451.)

16. Spence, I, 59.

17. See *Poems,* ed. Williams, I, 198 and *Anecdotes,* ed. Osborn, I, 59n.

supplying an ending to) and that by the latter he meant *begun at the beginning*. Actually they need not mean either, and could as well signify what Pope did with *Ep*. I. vii, that is, provide a missing fore-part to a poem first imitated in part only by Swift. What introduces the uncertainty is Pope's reference to an "Epistle," a designation which hardly fits *Sat*. II. vi, which is not an epistle but a satire (*sermo*) and so called in its title. I. vii, on the other hand, is an epistle, in fact as well as in title; and it alone of the two was published as "Imitated in the Manner of Dr. Swift."

It is likely that the attribution to *Sat*. II, vi has also been influenced by a letter from Bathurst to Swift, dated 5 October 1737, which apparently refers to the poem as an epistle:

That very pretty epistle which you writ many years ago to Lord Oxford, is printed incorrectly. I have a copy, of which I send you a transcript, which has some very good lines in it, that are not in the printed copy, and besides, if you will compare it with the original, you will find that you left off without going through with the epistle. The fable of the country and city mouse is as prettily told as anything of that kind ever was. . . .[18]

It is possible of course that Bathurst was simply confusing the two poems, both of which involve Harley, but only one of which is in fact an epistle and addressed "to a Noble Peer."[19] But to extrapolate from that a similar confusion on Pope's part seems hardly warranted on no better evidence than we have.

Though the imitations themselves afford no very decisive confirmation one way or the other, the balance seems to incline in the direction of the epistle as the poem alluded to. At first glance Pope's description of his effort as "familiar, lively, and with odd rhymes" would appear to fit one piece as well as the other, especially in respect to the odd rhymes:

18. Quoted in Butt, p. 248.
19. See *Poems*, ed. Williams, I, 169.

Satire II. vi	*Epistle* I. vii
below	sick
a-row	splenatick
before 'em	besiege ye
decorum	oblige ye
Spouse's	wherefore
Houses	care for
(you know)	advance
à propos	Ortolans
Fable	(enough for me)
hospitable	Independency
do't	a-row
coute qui coute	low
Treat	before you
tête à tête	Story

The satire goes on, though, to rhyme *law* and *ça, healing* and
Tail in, and (triplet fashion) *said, a-bed* and *red.* That Swift
proscribed the triplet could of course be made another argument
for this poem as the one he did not think "a right imitation of his
style," but then that would not tally with Pope's supposition that
he had "hit [Swift's] style exactly."

Actually, though in neither case does Pope achieve the essential Swift (how could he?), he comes closer to it by not a little in
the satire, with its macaronic rhyme, its fable, its homey flavor,
its merriment and lively pace. Swift might well have thought it
still short of him, but it is difficult to see how he could have
found it not *"at all* a right imitation of his style." The epistle, on
the other hand, is rather noticeably wide of the mark. Though
there are some "odd rhymes," they are not, as the comparison
shows, either so many or so egregious as those in the satire.
Familiar and lively to a point, the epistle possesses neither of
these qualities in the degree and extent of the satire, a fact no
doubt related to the double perspective remarked earlier as part

of its design. Except for a happy stroke here and there the epistle gets not much closer to Swift stylistically than its metre. It opens, as we have observed, on a note genuine enough, and the lines on the Weasel have the Swiftian ring, but stylistically the greater part of it is Pope in short metre:

> My Lord, your Favours well I know;
> 'Tis with Distinction you bestow.
>
> Scatter your Favours on a Fop,
> Ingratitude's the certain crop.
>
> The sprightly Wit, the lively Eye,
> Th'engaging Smile, the Gaiety.
>
> Sir, you may spare your Application
> I'm no such Beast, nor his Relation.[20]

Having approximated Swift's manner so relatively well in the satire, Pope may not have calculated the effect of the shifting design of the epistle upon its stylistic integrity and so found himself at a loss to understand Swift's failure to acknowledge the likeness. At any rate, left at the stand of conjecture, as we are in this question, it would seem that if Swift saw an imitation by Pope that did not hit his style at all, it was more likely *Ep.* I. vii than *Sat.* II. vi.

One reason for the neglect of these by-ventures in Pope's Horace is no doubt this very tendency to view them at face value merely, that is, as exercises in Swiftian imitation. As such they are interesting enough and show both Pope's adeptness and his limits in this kind of mimicry, but can hardly warrant serious notice. If one is to find them truly interesting or significant he must scan them for something besides Swift. He must, in a word, scan them for Pope.

Pope attached his name to neither imitation. He did not, we

---

20. Vv. 21–22, 31–32, 45–46, 59–60.

must suppose, partly in order to give them fair chance to pass for Swiftian, but also, it may be, in order to accommodate a hearing on other terms as well. In any event, the augmented *Sat.* II. vi was published with his characteristic ambiguity:

An/Imitation/Of The/Sixth Satire/Of The/Second Book/Of/ Horace./Hoc erat in Votis, &c./—/The first Part done in the Year 1714,/By Dr. Swift./The latter Part now first added,/And never before Printed./—/[21]

One effect of such a title of course, and probably one intent, is to suggest that what was not particularly called for, and so omitted, in 1714, is now, in 1738, apropos indeed, and so added: that this is how the poem would have ended had Swift himself, at this later date, undertaken its conclusion. The issue is not, in other words, as we have already observed, simply stylistic, but thematic as well.

I am, as I have said, inclined to agree with Harold Williams that vv. 9–28 of the augmented version are Swift's rather than Pope's, and to believe that Pope's part is confined to vv. 133 *ad fin.*[22] In these, though Pope hardly breathes the pure serene of Swift, he comes within range of that *aether* while at the same time he mediates between both climates—that of Horace and that of Swift alike—in such a way as to leave room for himself as well. When, for example, he adapts Horace's *cenaeque deum* (v. 65), he sets a table at once not un-Swiftian and distinctly Popeian:

> My Friends above, my Folks below,
> Chatting and laughing all-a-row,
> The Beans and Bacon set before 'em,
> The Grace-cup serv'd with all decorum:
> Each willing to be pleas'd, and please,
> And even the very Dogs at ease!   [135–140]

21. See Griffith, No. 479.
22. See *Poems*, ed. Williams, I, 197–98.

He has omitted Horace's Lar (*Larem*) and of course his slaves
(*vernas*), added "my Folks" to the Sabine friends (*ipse meique*),
made of *calices* a "Grace-cup," and addressed it with a "decorum" not hinted at in Horace, who rather suggests an absence of
same (*solutus/legibus insanis*). The dogs of course are Pope's.

The table talk that ensues Pope gives a political turn, which,
along with those parts of the tale of the country and city mice
that take the same bias, will be discussed later. Meanwhile, the
country fare, offered by the rural to the urban mouse, is bent in
the direction of the Dean:

> Pudding, that might have pleas'd a Dean;
> Cheese, such as men in Suffolk make,
> But wish'd it Stilton for his sake.   [166–168]

When the mice arrive at the home of the city-dweller, Pope,
in the vein of his earlier "Noons! and Nights divine!" follows
Horace in the spirit of mock solemnity, adapting nicely to the
decorative tastes of the mid-eighteenth century:

> Behold the place, where if a Poet
> Shin'd in Description, he might show it,
> Tell how the Moon-beam trembling falls
> And tips with silver all the walls:
> Palladian walls, Venetian doors,
> Grotesco roofs, and Stucco floors.   [187–192]

Where Horace's city mouse waits on the country mouse *vermili-
ter*, with the officiousness of a house-servant, Pope parades the
manners and speech of a gourmet:

> Tells all their names, lays down the law,
> *Que ça est bon! Ah goutez ça!*   [200–201]

The accent is Pope's, but the French is macaronic and Swiftian.
Horace is somewhere in the distance of signpost. In him this
scene of urban bliss is broken by a slamming door and barking

dogs (*valvarum strepitus . . . molossis personuit canibus*, vv.
112, 114–115). Pope augments the drama:

> No sooner said, but from the Hall
> Rush Chaplain, Butler, Dogs and all:
> 'A Rat, a Rat! Clap to the door—
> The Cat comes bouncing on the floor.   [210–213]

To which he adds a supplication in mock-heroics, with a witty
comic descent:

> O for the Heart of Homer's Mice,
> Or Gods to save them in a trice!
> (It was by Providence, they think,
> For your damn'd Stucco has no chink).   [214–217]

All of this is and is not Swiftian, is and is not Horatian, is and is
not Popeian. It is the happy conjunction of the three and the
opposition of them all. To judge it by any one of them alone is to
do it injustice and to miss its ingenuity and charm.

The ending of the episode picks up the political allusion, to
which we may now turn. The political significance of either
poem has not escaped notice, though it has never been ade-
quately canvassed. When Bowles annotated the "thin Court" of
Ep. I. vii. 12 as "Pope's usual topic of spleen and ridicule,"[23] he
indicated what must have been a general awareness in the
eighteenth century of the political dimension of both imitations,
though little has ever been made of it. One assumes that Professor Rogers points to it when he remarks that Pope's satires
between 1736 and 1738 were partly colored by his political
interests, and that in most of them he took occasion to animad-
vert upon Court and Ministry.[24] Pope's editors in The Scholars
Library observe of *Sat.* II. vi that

if it is read with the rest of the satires, and especially with Satire
II, ii . . . published four years earlier in 1734, one can see clearly

23. See Bowles, VI, 5.
24. Rogers, p. 75.

that for Pope the contrast between City extravagance and country simplicity held political and moral overtones that he did not wish to go unnoticed.[25]

Except for this, however, go unnoticed they do. Nor was it just overtones that Pope wished not to go unnoticed, but allusion, and he builds carefully in that fashion upon the cue with which Swift's part of the poem concludes: "Those Cares that haunt the Court and Town."

We have already observed that the political allusion begins early, with the table talk described in vv. 141 ff. Beginning with a harmless glance at the Italian songster so dear to Whig and Tory satirist alike, it quickly narrows to more partisan game. Horace's *de villis domibusve alienis* (v. 71) is given a turn unmistakably pointed.

> Here no man prates of idle things,
> How this or that Italian sings,
> A Neighbour's Madness, or his Spouse's,
> Or what's in either of the *Houses*.   [141–144]

With a facing text of *domibus* and *alienis* it is all but impossible to imagine Pope innocent, or his audience imperceptive, of allusion in the last verse to the Royal household with its mad King and Queen;[26] while "either of the *Houses*" would almost certainly carry the force of a double-edged pun, alluding on the one hand to the Houses of Parliament and on the other to the rival households of George II and Prince Frederick.[27] Pope, as we

25. Anthony Trott and Martin Axford, *Epistles and Satires of Alexander Pope* (London: Macmillan, 1964), pp. 153–154.

26. Though Pope would not scruple at *post mortem* allusion (cf. both dialogues of the *Epilogue*), the fact that Caroline died 20 November 1737 might be taken as evidence of composition prior to that date.

27. On 31 July 1737 the Prince removed the Princess (*enceinte*) to St. James's Palace so that their child should not be born under Royal roof (Hampton). By September 10 the Prince was ordered to remove from that residence and thereafter kept a separate court. See Hervey, Chaps. VII and

have seen, was already being drawn into the Opposition organiz-
ing itself around the Prince, by whom he had been done the
honor of a visit in 1735,[28] to whom he had done the honor of a
pup from Bounce,[29] and about whose separation from the King's
roof he made reference in a letter to Bethel 25 September 1737:
"I am glad by my rambles, to have escaped much of the disagree-
able noise, & the impertinent chatter of this place, about the
late Difference of the Courts."[30]

Such an interpretation suggests, in turn, more than idiomatic
significance in Pope's substitution of *scandal* and *Miser* for
Horace's neutral *malum* and *divitiis* in the lines immediately
following:

> But something much more our concern,
> And quite a scandal not to learn:
> Which is the happier, or the wiser,
> A man of Merit, or a Miser?   [145-148]

By the same token that invites association of *scandal* and *miser*
with the father (George), a "man of Merit" becomes the son
(Frederick), victim of paternal niggardliness as well as of paternal despotism.[31]

Characteristically, the allusion opens out from this centre in
the Royal family to embrace peerage, courtier, and finally patriotism, in an ever widening circle of indictment. It also capitalizes
the adaptability of Horace's fable to the town and country
constituency, real and symbolic alike, of Whig and Tory. What
we have in Pope's version of the fable is not just town mouse
and country mouse, but Whig mouse and Tory mouse.

VIII. Pope alludes more overtly to the separation when he locates (v. 184)
the city mouse in "a tall house near Lincoln's Inn," identified in E-C (III,
411n) as the house of the prince.

28. See letter to Bathurst 8 October: *Corr.*, III, 500.

29. Lyttelton to Pope 22 December 1736: *ibid.*, IV, 48.

30. *Ibid.*, IV, 86.

31. See Hervey, Chap. VI.

Where Horace puts his country mouse in a hole (*cavo*), Pope puts his at a "Board," and adds a glance at lordship:

> Receiv'd a Town Mouse at his Board,
> Just as a Farmer might a Lord.   [159–160]

That the farmer is Tory and the Lordship Whiggish becomes apparent as Pope subsequently refers to the city mouse as "Courtier" (vv. 171, 198) and gives him, with "his Breeding, and his Wit" (both ironically conferred), a jaunty and ultimately self-incriminatory speech:

> . . . "I vow you're mighty neat.
> "But Lord, my Friend, this savage Scene!
> "For God's sake, come, and live with Men:
> "Consider, Mice, like Men, must die,
> "Both small and great, both you and I:
> "Then spend your life in Joy and Sport,
> "(This doctrine, Friend, I learnt at Court.)   [174–180]

The speech is brilliantly complacent and self-deceptive, like those of the naïvely corrupt *adversarii* of the *Epilogue to the Satires*. The facile wisdom and flippant gaiety of its invitation scarcely disguise, for any save the speaker, the rankness of the Courtly doctrine and the arrogance of its professors. It is not surprising, then, that after the disaster of the urban surprisal the country mouse should cry out in a language suspiciously Caroline and Patriotic alike,

> "Give me again my hollow Tree!
> "A Crust of Bread, and Liberty.   [220–221]

Horace's mouse had spoken of *me silva cavusque,* my woods and hole. Pope has fused these, so to speak, into a royal oak, where another fugitive had sought refuge from pursuit. *Liberty* we recognize as the cry of Patriots since, in Bolingbroke's and Swift's and Pope's own time. Horace's mouse said nothing of it, though he did say something that perhaps Pope thought of as flavoring his allusion: *tutus ab insidiis,* especially if we take "insidious" in the modern sense.

As it turns out, the division of *Sat.* II. vi between Swift and Pope hit the case very well. The tale of the country mouse and city mouse was told in Horace by another, by Cervius, a country neighbor, wise about the city. Swift had done the part that pleased him most, the part of Horace, describing the blessings of the country (it was written at Letcombe, remember) and contrasting them to the disquiet of the city and the Court. Pope in turn, in keeping with his ethical mission of the thirties, took over the role of Cervius, supplying the fable that points the moral.[32] But he enriched that role, updating the observations about town and Court and allegorizing the fable on a principle of political allusion.

We have already touched on the poetic character of the *Epistle* in connection with its composition and the matter of Spenceian reference. Though it falls stylistically short of the Dean, even at times of Pope, it is not without quality, especially as it polarizes finally around the image of Pope himself—his moral resonance, his pride and modesty alike, and his resolution. We have remarked how well he began, achieving something not only of Swift, but of Horace and himself as well: " 'Tis true, my Lord, I gave my word," etc. Except for a happy stroke here and there—like the nicely trimmed couplet of "Splenatik" and the Butterflies of "first warm Weather"—he is perhaps up to none of these standards in the verses intervening between the opening and those that introduce the "Constitution" of his past and present. The anecdote of the Weasel, as we have said, catches the spirit of Swift nicely, and with it we are home free, for the rest is Pope:

> Extremely ready to resign
> All that may make me none of mine.

32. Pope of course ascribes the tale to Prior, but this may be just another element in his subterfuge about his hand in the imitation.

South-sea Subscriptions take who please,
Leave me but Liberty and Ease.
'Twas what I said to Craggs and Child,
Who prais'd my Modesty, and smil'd.
Give me, I cry'd, (enough for me)
My Bread, and Independency!
So bought an Annual Rent or two.
And liv'd—just as you see I do;
Near fifty, and without a Wife,
I trust that sinking Fund, my Life.
Can I retrench? Yes, mighty well,
Shrink back to my Paternal Cell,
A little House, with Trees a-row,
And like its Master, very low,
There dy'd my Father, no man's Debtor,
And there I'll die, nor worse nor better.

There are few lines more pleasing to be found in Pope, and it is a tribute to his great talent that he could achieve their quality in octosyllabics—octosyllabics that are not at all Swiftian, but wholly Popeian and wholly satisfying.

Political allusion in the *Epistle* is, as we have already seen, of a rather more subtle kind than in the *Satire*, depending mainly on the evocation of a Harleian past in contrast to a Hanoverian present, and given its first explicit notice in the pun on "Constitution." While on the whole it remains implicit, there are certain other more or less overt signals of its presence, as in the political turn Pope gives Horace's *otia* . . . *liberrima*, ease and freedom (v. 36):

> Extremely ready to resign
> All that may make me none of mine,
> South-sea Subscriptions take who please,
> Leave me but Liberty and Ease.

The reference to Craggs, which follows, must be understood also to call up more than the fact that, as Warburton pointed out, "Craggs gave him some South-sea subscriptions," which Pope

was careless of.[33] It could scarcely have failed to recall Pope's
published sentiments on at least three occasions regarding
Craggs as statesman: the verses on him in *To Mr. Addison,
Occasioned by his Dialogues on Medals* (1720), the *Epitaph on
James Craggs, Esq.* (1727), which repeats the lines in the
Addison, and the *Epistle to James Craggs, Esq.* (1735). In the
first two Craggs is celebrated as

> Statesman, yet Friend to Truth! of Soul sincere,
> In Action faithful, and in Honour clear!
> Who broke no promise, serv'd no private end,
> Who gain'd no Title, and who lost no Friend,
> Ennobled by Himself, by All approv'd,
> Prais'd, wept, and honour'd, by the Muse he lov'd.[34]

The *Epistle to Craggs* adds to such sentiments:

> All this thou wert; and being this before,
> Know, Kings and Fortune cannot make thee more.
> Then scorn to gain a Friend by servile ways,
> Nor wish to lose a Foe these Virtues raise;
> But candid, free, sincere, as you began,
> Proceed!—a Minister, but still a Man;
> Be not (exalted to whate'er degree)
> Asham'd of any Friend, nor ev'n of Me.[35]

Such attributes, belonging not just to a man but to an era since
departed, are precisely those that Pope's part of the epistle
deplores, by implication and by allusion, the want of in 1738.
    The last such suggestion of political relevance is the witty
reference to "that sinking Fund, my Life," to which the poet

33. See Butt, 272, note to v. 267.
34. See Ault, *Minor Poems*, 281–282.
35. *Ibid.*, p. 210. Pope had alluded to Craggs only a little before the first of
these Swiftian imitations, in the *Epistle to Murray*, v. 45, obviously with the
same patriotic implications. See above, pp. 78–79.

would rather trust than Sir Robert's,[36] and with which he takes his leave of that Pagod for his Paternal Cell.

We have too long invoked the wrong password to Pope's imitations "In the Manner of Dr. Swift." The shibboleth, it seems, is not stylistic after all, but political. The style is but the awkward and visible sign by which we are directed to the true Swift of the parody—not the Swift of nimble numbers, but of political sun and shadow. It is in *this* sign that Pope turns otherwise certain defeat into conquest.[37]

36. Cf. W. T. Selley, *England in the Eighteenth Century* (London: A. & C. Black, 1934), p. 43.

37. It has perhaps not gone unnoticed that Pope's part of the epistle assumes an elegiac quality not paralleled in Horace, who, though he wittily admits he is *non qualis erat bonae sub regno Cynarae,* is not in a solemn mood at all. Pope, on the contrary, adopts a tone and diction that makes of his part something like a political elegy.

6

Epilogue:
Receit to Make a Satire

POPE never left a receit to make a satire, as he did, face-tiously, to make an epic poem. What he thought about satire and the satirist must therefore be pieced together from his practice and from his more or less scattered comment on the subject. From these sources one thing emerges with immediate and striking clarity, and that is his sense of the dignity of satire. Pope is, in fact, the only great satirist to take an emphatic and convincing stand on this point. For him satire was not only a calling, but a high calling. "Rev'rent I touch thee!" is the way he put it in the *Epilogue to the Satires:*

> O sacred Weapon! left for Truth's defence,
> Sole Dread of Folly, Vice, and Insolence!
> To all but Heav'n-directed hands deny'd,
> The Muse may give thee, but the Gods must guide.[1]

This tells us even more. Because it is both sacred and divinely prompted, satire functions as a scourge of God. But it is also poetry, the gift of the Muse, and for that reason too something exceptional, above scurrility and abuse, libel and lampoon, as he

1. Dialogue ii. 212–216.

makes clear in the verses leading up to the portrait of Sporus in the *Epistle to Dr Arbuthnot:* "Curst be the Verse" that, among other things, makes "Satire a Lampoon, and Fiction, Lye." As an ethical agency, satire has standards appropriate to that office:

> Hence Satire rose, that just the medium hit,
> And heals with Morals what it hurts with Wit.[2]

As a poem, it is as much a child of the Muses as any other, and Pope likes to think of his satire as "Song."[3]

But for all its dignity, Pope's concept of satire was not unrealistic. Pope had not Addison's fastidious dislike of ridicule, or his unwillingness to venture for it, content rather to

> Damn with faint praise, assent with civil leer,
> And without sneering, teach the rest to sneer;
> Willing to wound, and yet afraid to strike,
> Just hint a fault, and hesitate dislike.[4]

Pope is, in fact, emphatic in his commitment to the "Pow'r" of satire to "hurt,"[5] and to do so openly and by virtue of particularity and personal reference. Arbuthnot found this tendency alarming and counseled prudence, begging Pope to "study more to reform than chastise. . . ."[6] To which Pope replied:

To reform and not to chastise, I am afraid is impossible. . . . To attack Vices in the abstract, without touching Persons, may be safe fighting . . . but it is fighting with Shadows. General propositions are obscure, misty, and uncertain, compar'd with plain, full, and home examples: Precepts only apply to our Reason, which in most men is but weak: Examples are pictures, and strike the Senses, nay

2. *Epistle to Augustus,* vv. 261–262.
3. Cf. *Epilogue to the Satires,* ii. 9. Also *Arbuthnot,* v. 341 and *Augustus,* v. 395. For satire as child of the Muse, see *Epilogue to the Satires,* ii. 223 and *passim.*
4. *Epistle to Arbuthnot,* vv. 201–204.
5. *Sat.* II. i. 85.
6. See *Corr.,* III, 417.

raise the Passions, and call in those (the strongest and most general of all motives) to the aid of reformation. Every vicious man makes the case his own; and that is the only way by which such men can be affected, much less deterr'd. So that to chastise is to reform.[7]

As he had already written to Gay (16 December 1731),

Some fancy, that to say a Thing is *Personal,* is the same as to say it is *Injust,* not considering, that nothing can be *Just* that is not *Personal:* I am afraid that all such Writings and Discourses as touch no Man, will mend no Man.[8]

For which reason, as he tells Burlington, he is inclined to forego the use of "Fictitious" for "*Real* Names," because only then can justice be assured and satire made certain of its aim.[9] He conducts the same argument in Dialogue ii of the *Epilogue to the Satires.*

Pope's theory of satire, in this respect, is a correlative of his theory of human nature, in which, though reason is the standard, passion is the motive force, and acts most readily upon the promptings of sense. By its home thrust—its aim at the person and the particular crime—satire can achieve reason's work by *forcing* the transition from self-love to social on the most cogent argument of all, the aversion to pain. Pope respected reason; he tried to base his life upon it; but he also knew its limitations, and its need, from time to time, of passion's prod.[10] Hence satire, and hence the satirist.

Nor is Pope willing to limit the reach of satire. In the *Epilogue* he insists upon the prerogative of satire to reach as high as the crime. The adversary tries to get the satirist to spare the Court. "Down, down, proud Satire!" cries the poet, in ironic assent,

7. *Ibid.,* p. 419.
8. *Ibid.,* p. 255.
9. *Ibid.,* p. 266.
10. Cf. *Essay on Man,* Epistle II.

> . . . tho' a Realm be spoil'd,
> Arraign no mightier Thief than wretched *Wild,*
> Or if a Court or Country's made a Job,
> Go drench a Pick-pocket, and join the Mob.[11]

But no. "A Knave's a Knave, to me, in ev'ry State," as he said in the *Epistle to Dr Arbuthnot.*

Related to this attitude is Pope's view of the satirist as a man of courage—the courage of his calling, the courage of his convictions, and the courage that the word itself specifies, the heart that disdains fear.

> Truth guards the Poet, sanctifies the line,
> And makes Immortal, Verse as mean as mine.
>
> Ask you what Provocation I have had?
> The strong Antipathy of Good to Bad.
>
> Not proud, nor servile, be one Poet's praise
> That, if he pleas'd, he pleas'd by manly ways.
>
> That not in Fancy's Maze he wander'd long,
> But stoop'd to Truth, and moraliz'd his song.
> That not for Fame, but Virtue's better end,
> He stood the furious Foe, the timid Friend.[12]

Pope's own courage is contagious; it is *encouraging.* As such it is not only admirable in itself, but a real part of his satiric economy.

Of the style of satire Pope had little to say. Spence records his observation that Oldham was "indelicate," "too rough and coarse," that though he had "strong rage" (presumably a virtue), it was "too much like Billingsgate."[13] Though Rochester had

---

11. *Epilogue to the Satires,* ii. 38–41.

12. See, in turn, *Epilogue,* ii. 246–247; 197–98; and *Epistle to Arbuthnot,* vv. 336–337, 340–343. And cf. *Sat.* II. i, *passim.*

13. Spence, I, 202.

"more delicacy," he had not "so much delicacy or exactness as Dorset. . . ."[14] Dryden, he told Spence, "always uses proper language: lively, natural, and fitted to the subject. 'Tis scarce ever too high or too low—never perhaps, except in his plays."[15] Of himself he admits only,

> I love to pour out all myself, as plain
> As downright *Shippen,* or as old *Montagne.*
>
> My Head and Heart thus flowing thro' my Quill,
> Verse-man or Prose-man, term me which you will.[16]

He will, on the other hand, occasionally affect a standard of epistolary gravity which he does not often practice, if ever really. "I have not the courage," he wrote to Swift (20 April 1733),

> to be such a Satyrist as you, but I would be as much, or more, a Philosopher. You call your satires, Libels; I would rather call my satires, Epistles: They will consist more of morality than wit, and grow graver, which you will call duller. I shall leave it to my Antagonists to be witty (if they can) and content myself to be useful, and in the right.[17]

What we find here, in reality, is the tension between Pope's respect for the ethical dignity of satire and his own peculiar genius for wit and edge—a genius which found, as we have seen, endorsement on the theoretical level as well, in his theory of the place of the passions in satire's rational goals. We know, in fact, that Pope's style, like his temperament, is keen and forthright, though never shrill or unnatural. Or perhaps it would be truer to say that his style, like his temperament, is *ardent,* warm alike in love or hate.[18] The stylistic counterpart of his objection

---

14. *Ibid.*
15. *Ibid.,* p. 24.
16. *Sat.* II. i. 51–52, 63–64.
17. *Corr.,* III, 366. Cf. *Sat.* II. i. 151.
18. As "warm," he says in *Epistle* I. i. 30, "as true."

to Addison's temperamental deficiency is his characterization of Hervey's expressive insipidity—his merely annoying *buzz*, his Spaniel-like *mumbling* of his game, his "florid Impotence": "Wit that can creep, and Pride that licks the dust."

In the *Epistle to Augustus*, where he speaks of the English poets, Pope takes exception to Spenser's archaic style, to Sidney's halting verse, to Milton's occasional flats, and to the barrenness of wit in the verse of "The Mob of Gentlemen who wrote with Ease." He praises Addison's pure page, Swift's wit, Waller's smoothness, and Dryden's "full resounding line,/The long majestic march, and energy divine." He speaks of correctness, censures the "pert low Dialogue" of Farquhar, the lack of "grace" in Van, and deplores the spectacle of stage farce. As for the English Pindar,

> Who now reads Cowley? if he pleases yet
> His moral pleases, not his pointed wit;
> Forgot his Epic, nay Pindaric Art,
> But still I love the language of his Heart.[19]

I quote these lines because that is the language Pope always loved, the language he prided himself on: "My Head and Heart thus flowing thro' my Quill."[20] It is somewhere near the secret of his own stylistic genius—that ardency we have spoken of—and it is close too to what he acknowledges as the virtue of Dryden's style: "lively, natural, and fitted to the subject." But intermixed with that is something also of Dryden's "energy divine," a heightening of the accent as the satiric pulse mounts. Pope's style, fundamentally a speaking idiom, prompted by a warmth as

19. Vv. 75–78. See also vv. 97–114, 215–216, 221–224, 267–269, 288–289, and 304 ff.

20. I am using "language of the Heart" in a different sense of course from that Pope intends here, where it is a metaphor for Cowley's *sentiments* or moral ideas. I use it to describe Pope's fondness for what may be called the voice of candor.

genial as it is aggressive, ranges from its center in the middle style to reaches above and below that norm. It is, as we shall see, the expression of a personality.

Insofar as he speaks of the matter, then, Pope expresses a view of satire as ultimately heroic and inspired, as a public guardian and hence an art and conscience superior to libel and lampoon; but dependent, even so, for its effectiveness, upon wit, personal example, sensory and passional arousal; without bounds as to target, spoken freely in a style now grave, now gay, but essentially colloquial, with the power to sing as well as to curse, and with the heart to do both.

From Pope's practice, which confirms all of this, we can deduce still more. If we approach it statistically, we discover, for example, that he wrote few satires (I am not counting the burlesques or the *Essay on Man*) of his own invention. Among the satires so-called, only three out of a total of nine are originals: the two dialogues of the *Epilogue* and the fragment 1740. Of his epistles (all more or less satiric), exactly one half are originals (the *Arbuthnot* and the four *Ethic Epistles*), and half are imitations of Horace. In all, then, something less than half of his total satiric output of this kind is original in the sense of having no specific model; slightly more than half is imitative. From this we may deduce that for Pope originality of "fable," so to speak, was no more important than it was, say, for Shakespeare. Both knew that human nature is unchanging, and that originality in its portrayal lies not, therefore, in the invention of vehicles, but in adapting those fables of old (discovered, not devised) to the demands of their own age and genius. Where Pope does invent, it is always "something like Horace." Horace and Nature were, he had found, the same.

Pope's themes reflect this fact, while at the same time they reflect his responsible and sensitive view of satire. His most recurrent theme is satire itself, its necessity, its nature, its nobility. Following Horace he also writes on the priority of the art of living to the art of poetry,[21] a profession which we need not suspect in him any more than we do in Horace. Under the same inspiration he writes on the virtues of the simple, or country, life, as against the venality and viciousness of the city.[22] Akin to this is his imitation of Donne's Second, on the corrupt town; Horace's *Sat.* II. ii, on the art of plain living; and Donne's Fourth, "The Impertinent," itself adapted from Horace's *Sat.* I. ix, *Ibam forte via sacra.* Corruption in the Realm is the subject of the fragment *1740*, as it is of others, including the *Epilogue to the Satires. Epistle* I. vi follows Horace on the theme *nil admirari,* with a touch of the vanity of human wishes as that relates, in especial, to "Pow'r and Place." *Sat.* I. ii follows Horace on adultery. Related to it are *Ethic Epistles* I and II (*Cobham* and *To a Lady*), studies in the characters of men and women. *Ethic Epistles* III and IV treat of the use and abuse of riches. Pope everywhere of course, in the Varronian poems and in the didactic poems (*Essay on Criticism, Essay on Man*), attacks human pride. Pope's themes, it is important to note, are never merely personal, though his treatment is largely so. Nor is he characteristically interested (as Addison was) in foibles and follies. His themes tend rather to public and private vices and virtues: the art of living, the disgrace of living, and the necessity of satire in order to promote the one and discourage the other.

Pope's practice also reveals his predilection for the dramatic immediacy and conviction of personal address. He employs dialogue in four of his pieces (*Sat.* II. i, *Arbuthnot,* and the two dialogues of the *Epilogue*), an embedded or reported dialogue in the imitation of Donne's Fourth; and the epistolary form in ten instances, including the *Ethic Epistles.* Only four of the satires are more or less monologic (II. ii, I. ii, II. vi, and Donne's

21. Cf. *Ep.* II. ii and I. i.
22. Cf. *Sat.* II. vi and *Ep.* I. vii. Pope has in mind a Hanoverian city. He is not to be thought of as in *romantic* revolt against urban life.

Second), and of these one makes use of the nonce adversary (II. vi) and one of the satiric prolocutor (II. ii). Though his practice is not, like Juvenal's, strictly decisive, with the Roman's clear-cut preference for the monologue, Pope plainly prefers an informal address, either a conversation with one present (dialogue) or a talk, on paper, with one not present (though often addressed as if he were—the epistle). Pope rarely lectures an audience. He would rather leave that to a Bethel.

As we have remarked, Pope favored personal satire over abstract, example over precept, *pathos* over reasoning. It is only in the *Dunciad,* however, that he contents himself with featuring mean subjects; in his Lucilian satire his prime targets are men and women of rank, such as Hervey, Walpole, Lady Mary, and even the Royal family. But as he said, "Scriblers or Peers, alike are *Mob* to me" (*Sat.* II. i. 140), and so his satire balks at neither extreme. What is more, it does not, typically, limit itself to one or the other in any given instance. His formal satire characteristically ranges the social spectrum, herding together the Bentleys and Bufos, Curlls and Chartres, Lintots and Lord Fannys, Dennises and Duchesses, Tibbalds and Timons. These are, after all, birds of a feather; they complement each other and their presence together confirms Pope's conviction that corruption at the top breeds corruption at the bottom:

> Ye Gods! shall *Cibber's* Son, without rebuke
> Swear like a Lord? or a *Rich* out-whore a Duke?
> A fav'rite's *Porter* with his Master vie,
> Be brib'd as often, and as often lie?[23]

The same circumstances illustrate how, at the same time, by a circular principle, the high stoop to the low, and so subvert the ancient standard:

> See, all our Nobles begging to be Slaves!
> See, all our Fools aspiring to be Knaves![24]

23. *Epilogue to the Satires,* i. 115–118.
24. *Ibid.,* vv. 163–164.

More often than not Pope will call his lower characters by real name, his higher ones by fictitious, though he does not hesitate to call a Montagu a Montagu, a Cornus Sir Robert, or a King and Queen George and Caroline. Less often, much less in fact, will he call a Welsted *Pitholeon* (*Arbuthnot*, v. 9), an Aphra Behn *Astraea* (*Ep*. II. i. 290), and an Oldfield *Narcissa* (*Cobham*, v. 243). Though something of legal precaution doubtless influenced the fictitious names in high place, the fact that Pope did, as we have seen, use real ones as well, shows that this was not an over-riding consideration in his practice. The real reason must lie more nearly in his supposition that, in general, allusive names (Cornus, Fanny, Sappho) were both more appropriate and more damning to the high estate, while their own names (Curll, Lintot, Tibbald), by virtue of their popular fame and, occasionally, sound, were a more effective appellation for the common lot.[25] Finally, it is worth noting, Pope does not often invoke the dash for names, using it more as a tease than as an evasion, for initial and terminal letters nearly always appear to point the way to the intervals between. Whatever, in short, Pope did with names in satire, he seems to have been governed by satiric rather than prudential criteria.

Pope's use of persons and names in satire is not confined however to victims. His satires are also filled with the names of good and noble men (and women), who serve not only as foils to his villains, but as genuine objects of approbation. "To VIRTUE ONLY and HER FRIENDS, A FRIEND," "God knows," he says, "I

25. On Pope's use of names see Maynard Mack, " 'Wit and Poetry and Pope': Some Observations on his Imagery," in *Pope and His Contemporaries,* ed. James L. Clifford and Louis A. Landa (Oxford: Clarendon, 1949), pp. 26–28. Also Aubrey Williams, *Pope's Dunciad, A Study of its Meaning* (Baton Rouge: Louisiana State University Press, 1955), pp. 65–68. One must recognize of course that it was customary to refer to commoners by their surnames, but not so to persons of rank or aristocracy, though their titles might be used (*viz.,* Burlington). But Pope had arguments more relative than decorum for his practice in this regard.

praise a Courtier where I can": St. John, Queensberry, Craggs, Scarborough, Wyndham, Polwarth, Lyttelton, and many others, including even, upon occasion, Sir Robert. Other laudatory names and portraits throng his verses too, like those of Bethel, Gay, Swift, Arbuthnot, his father and mother, and, not least, his own:

> Not Fortune's Worshipper, nor Fashion's Fool,
> Not Lucre's Madman, nor Ambition's Tool,
> Not proud, nor servile, be one Poet's praise
> That, if he pleas'd, he pleas'd by manly ways.[26]

More than any satirist before him, Pope brings his norm to the fore by means of panegyrical portraits and vignettes.[27]

That Pope himself figures among these panegyrical characters suggests another, and quite important, aspect of his practice of satire, and that is his strong sense of himself as satirist. Pope is not merely interested in the ethical proof of his moral and literary worth, the *ethos* which is partly a convention, partly a necessity, of the satirist; he is alive to himself as a personality, and his satires breathe the charm and force alike of his real presence:

> I nod in Company, I wake at Night,
> Fools rush into my Head, and so I write.

> Content with little, I can piddle here
> On Broccoli and mutton, round the year.

26. *Epistle to Arbuthnot,* vv. 334–337. Pope rarely includes himself by name of course, though he will sometimes do so in an oblique and playful way, as he does in vv. 235–236 of the *Epistle to Augustus:* "Verse chears their leisure, Verse assists their work,/Verse prays for Peace, or sings down Pope and Turk." Pope knew that there was more than one Catholic villain by that name.

27. Dryden frequently does this too and he may have been influential on Pope's practice of it.

Shut, shut the door, good *John!* fatigu'd I said,
Tye up the knocker, say I'm sick, I'm dead.

For Right Hereditary tax'd and fin'd,
He stuck to Poverty with Peace of Mind;
And me, the Muses help'd to undergo it;
Convict a Papist He, and I a Poet.

Besides, a fate attends on all I write,
That when I aim at praise, they say I bite.

As drives the storm, at any door I knock,
And house with Montagne now, or now with Lock.

Kept Dross for Duchesses, the world shall know it,
To you gave Sense, Good-humour, and a Poet.[28]

It is this impression of personality, as opposed to role, that
crowns Pope's satiric mastery and distinctness. It is a mistake
therefore, I believe, to lay too much emphasis upon the idea of a
persona, vir bonus or whatever, as the spokesman of his satire.
Some such mechanism unquestionably plays a part, and we are
fortunate in the reminder of its sanctuary from many of the
fallacies of older criticism, but in the last analysis the voice we
hear in a Popeian satire is that, not of a mask, but of a real
personality, and that is a conspicuous factor in its appeal and
impact.

Though it is doubtless unnecessary to observe that Pope's
satire is expressed almost exclusively in the decasyllabic couplet, it may not be amiss to remark that that fact in itself
constitutes a very nearly unique phenomenon in English satire
to his time. With the exception of Dryden, who wrote only one
Lucilian satire (*The Medal*), the Restoration satirists employed

---

28. *Sat.* II. i. 13–14; *Sat.* II. ii. 137–138; *Arbuthnot*, vv. 1–2; *Ep.* II. ii.
64–67; *Augustus*, vv. 408–409; *Ep.* I. i. 25–26; *To a Lady*, vv. 291–292. Cf.
also the stunning self-portraits in the *Epistle to Arbuthnot*.

a variety of verse and stanza forms for satire, a consequence, in turn, of the greater variety of satire practiced, most of it of a lower order—lampoon, low burlesque, and the like. A similar tendency toward variety of form, though less prolific, succeeds on Pope. But with the exception of two poems written in imitation of Swift's octosyllabics (*Sat.* II. vi and *Ep.* I. vii), Pope wrote serious satire exclusively in decasyllabics, not as a rule really heroic, like Dryden's, but a flexible middle sort, touching both higher and lower registers. There is no need either to discuss the extraordinary manner in which Pope sophisticated the rhetoric and metre of the couplet, so completely identifying it with himself and with satire that it has never since served another master or another genre.[29]

Pope's receit for satire is built upon his view of the genre as at once sacred and secular, poetic and plain spoken. If the ends are ideal, the means are quite real, though never therefore merely crude or flat. Still, an ounce of pain is worth a pound of precept in the Popeian view, and the pungency of personality the only sure way to a bad man's stomach. His dish will serve a prince as readily as a pauper, and his table caters to both. Nothing exotic and nothing sordid, but proven fare, served up with verve—and what's more rare, a Poet to say grace. No abstraction, but a Poet, as real as his friends and foes, as genial as he is severe, as courageous as they come.

29. For the rhetoric of Pope's couplet one should consult especially the work of Tillotson and Wimsatt.

Index

WITHDRAWN